A Green Place

A Green Place
Modern Poems

compiled by
WILLIAM JAY SMITH

illustrated by Jacques Hnizdovsky

A Merloyd Lawrence Book
DELACORTE PRESS / SEYMOUR LAWRENCE

A MERLOYD LAWRENCE BOOK
Published by
Delacorte Press/Seymour Lawrence
1 Dag Hammarskjold Plaza
New York, N.Y. 10017

Manufactured in the United States of America
First printing

Designed by Judith Neuman

The compiler of A GREEN PLACE and Delacorte Press/Seymour Lawrence wish to thank the following authors, publishers, and agents for permission to reprint copyrighted material. Every possible effort has been made to trace the ownership of each poem included. If any errors or omissions have occurred, correction will be made in subsequent printings, provided that the publisher is notified of their existence. • "Song from a Country Fair" by Léonie Adams. •Reprinted by permission of the author. • "Reflection: After Visiting Old Friends" and "Okeechobee" by John Allison. "Reflection: After Visiting Old Friends" first appeared in *Black Warrior Review*, Copyright 1974 by *Black Warrior Review*. Reprinted by permission of John Allison and *Black Warrior Review*. • "The Visit" by A. R. Ammons is reprinted from COLLECTED POEMS 1951–1971 by A. R. Ammons by permission of W. W. Norton & Company, Inc. Copyright © 1972 by A. R. Ammons. • "Travelling Companions" by Richard Armour in *The New Yorker* © 1956. Reprinted by permission. • "Night Mail" by W. H. Auden. Copyright 1938 by W. H. Auden. Reprinted from W. H. AUDEN: COLLECTED POEMS edited by Edward Mendelson by permission of Random House, Inc. and Faber & Faber Ltd. • "Snow" by Mary Austin from THE CHILDREN SING IN THE FAR WEST by Mary Austin. Copyright 1928 by Mary Austin. Copyright renewed 1956 by Kenneth M. Chapman and Mary C. Wheelwright. Reprinted by permission of Houghton Mifflin Company. • "The Flood" and "The Blue Hole" by Charles G. Bell from *Delta Return* (Indiana University Press, 1956). Copyright 1954 by Charles G. Bell. Reprinted by permission of the author. • "A Sympathy, A Welcome" by John Berryman. This poem originally appeared in *The New Yorker*. Reprinted by permission of Kate Berryman. • "World Winter" by Earle Birney from THE COLLECTED POEMS OF EARLE BIRNEY. Reprinted by permission of the Canadian publishers, McClelland and Stewart Limited, Toronto. • "Reading in Fall Rain" by Robert Bly from THIS TREE WILL BE HERE FOR A THOUSAND YEARS by Robert Bly. Copyright © 1979 by Robert Bly. Reprinted by permission of Harper & Row, Publishers, Inc. • "To an Artist, to Take Heart" and "Packet of Letters" by Louise Bogan from THE BLUE ESTUARIES by Louise Bogan. Copyright 1936, 1937 by *The New Yorker*. Copyright renewed © 1964 by Louise Bogan. These poems first appeared in *The New Yorker*. Reprinted by permission of Farrar, Straus & Giroux, Inc. • "The Round" by Philip Booth from THE ISLANDERS by Philip Booth. Copyright © 1952, 1957, 1958, 1959, 1960, 1961 by Philip Booth. Reprinted by permission of Viking Penguin Inc. • "The Bean Eaters" by Gwendolyn Brooks from THE WORLD OF GWENDOLYN BROOKS by Gwendolyn Brooks. Copyright © 1959 by Gwendolyn Brooks. "Narcissa" (text only) by Gwendolyn Brooks from BRONZEVILLE BOYS AND GIRLS by Gwendolyn Brooks. Copyright © 1956 by Gwendolyn Brooks Blakely. Reprinted by permission of Harper & Row, Publishers, Inc. • "Bouquet in Dog Time" by Hayden Carruth. Reprinted by permission of the author. • "On a Sea-Grape Leaf" by Katherine Garrison Chapin. Reprinted by permission of Edmund R. Biddle. • "Some Sound Advice from Singapore" by John Ciardi from FAST AND SLOW by John Ciardi. Copyright © 1975 by John Ciardi. Reprinted by permission of Houghton Mifflin Company. • "Good Times" by Lucille Clifton from GOOD TIMES by Lucille Clifton. Copyright © 1969 by Lucille Clifton. Reprinted by permission of Random House, Inc. • "Time Piece" by William Cole. © 1967 by William Cole. Reprinted by permission of the author. • "The Wall of China" by Padraic Colum. Reprinted by permission of the Estate of Padraic Colum. • "Electricity is Funny!" by John Currier from *The Hollins Critic*, vol. VII, no. 2, April 1970. Copyright © by John Currier. Reprinted by permission of Denise Cobham Currier. • "About Motion Pictures" by Ann Darr. Copyright © 1968 by Ann Darr. "Love Is" by Ann Darr. Copyright © 1970 by Ann Darr. Both poems are from ST. ANN'S GUT (1971) by Ann Darr. Reprinted by permission of William Morrow & Company. • "Magpie" by Peter Davison from THE CITY AND THE ISLAND. Copyright © 1966 by Peter Davison (New York: Atheneum, 1966). Reprinted by permission of Atheneum Publishers. • "The Wind Has Wings" an Eskimo chant translated by Raymond de Coccola and Paul King from AYORAMA by Raymond de Coccola and Paul King. © Oxford University Press. Reprinted by permission of Oxford University Press (Canada). • "Miss T" and "Bunches of Grapes" by Walter de la Mare. Reprinted by permission of the Literary Trustees of Walter de la Mare and the Society of Authors as their representative. • "The Fisher Cat" by Richard Eberhart from FIELDS OF GRACE by Richard Eberhart. Copyright © 1972 by Richard Eberhart. Reprinted by permission of Oxford University Press, Inc. • "Sonnet: Dolce Stil Novo" by Gavin Ewart. Reprinted by permission of the author. • "The Snowfish" by Edward Field from STAND UP, FRIEND, WITH ME. Copyright © 1963 by Edward Field. Reprinted by permission of Grove Press, Inc. • "Cobb Would Have Caught It" by Robert Fitzgerald from IN THE ROSE OF TIME by Robert Fitzgerald. Copyright 1943 by Robert Fitzgerald. Reprinted by permission of New Directions Publishing Corporation. • "August Song on Perry Street" by Lloyd Frankenberg in *The New Yorker* © 1954. Reprinted by permission. • "I'll Tell You What a Flapper Is" by Anne Hobson Freeman first published in *The New Virginia Review*, volume one, 1979; Copyright © 1979 by Anne Hobson Freeman. Reprinted by permission of the author and *The New Virginia Review*. • "Questioning Faces," "Stopping by Woods on a Snowy Evening," "Nothing Gold Can Stay," and "The Last Word of a Bluebird" by Robert Frost from

Library of Congress Cataloging in Publication Data
Main entry under title:
A green place.
"A Merloyd Lawrence book."
Includes indexes.
Summary: A collection of modern poetry on a variety of subjects and in a variety of forms from simple rhymes to complex stanzaic patterns.
1. Children's poetry. [1. Poetry—Collections]   I. Smith, William Jay, 1918–   .   II. Hnizdovsky, Jacques, 1915–   , ill.
PN6109.97.G7   808.81'088054   82-2363
ISBN 0-440-02920-1   AACR2

To
the memory of
Louise Bogan

CONTENTS

INTRODUCTION

I once prepared as a school project a notebook on poetry. On the cover I pasted the picture of a majestic carved gate that I had cut from a magazine, and to the top of the gate I attached a bright feather; inside my notebook I copied out my favorite poems and the definitions of poetry by a number of great poets. I realize now that my cover was itself my own definition, for poetry is indeed a splendid gateway to intense and rewarding experience, offering, throughout one's life, "magnificence within a frame."

Our first view of that magnificence is in nursery rhymes. Dylan Thomas speaks for all of us when he tells of falling in love with their words: "What the words stood for, symbolized, or meant, was of very secondary importance; what mattered was the *sound* of them as I heard them for the first time on the lips of the remote and incomprehensible grown-ups who seemed, for some reason, to be living in my world. And these words were, to me, as the notes of bells, the sounds of musical instruments, the noises of wind, sea, and rain, the rattle of milkcarts, the clopping of hooves on cobbles, the fingering of branches on a windowpane might be to someone, deaf from birth, who has miraculously found his hearing. . . . They made their own original associations as they sprang and shone."

I have chosen to call this collection of modern poems, which I have compiled over many years, *A Green Place*. I take the title from a poem of my own, in which a place is imagined that is eternally green, made up of parts of our world, but wholly new and different. It is such a place that poetry, composed of words that spring and shine, can always offer us. It is such a place that I had pictured beyond the carved gate of my notebook.

The poems in this collection were written almost entirely in the twentieth century. I have included a few poems written in the nineteenth century because they seem thoroughly modern in spirit. There are poems on a variety of subjects and in a variety of forms, all the way from simple rhymes to complex stanzaic patterns, some of which were first used hundreds of years ago. There are also poems composed in free verse, not employing regular meters but relying rather on subtle musical cadences. Some of these poems were written by the most famous poets in the world today; others are the work of young poets who are published here for the first time. Some were written in Africa and Australia; others are translated from French, German, and even, in one instance, from Hungarian. Some are solemn and tragic in tone; some are light and funny. All of them will, I hope, in one way or another, by demonstrating the magnificent possibilities of language, lead to poetry's green place.

—W. J. S.

A GREEN PLACE

I know a place all fennel-green and fine
Far from the white icecap, the glacial flaw,
Where shy mud hen and dainty porcupine
Dance in delight by a quivering pawpaw;

Dance by catalpa tree and flowering peach
With speckled guinea fowl and small raccoon,
While the heron, from his perforated beach,
Extends one bony leg beyond the moon.

I know a place so green and fennel-fine
Its boundary is air; and will you come?
A bellflower tinkles by a trumpet vine,
A shrouded cricket taps a midget drum.

There blue flies buzz among the wild sweet peas;
The water speaks: black insects pluck the stream.
May apples cluster there by bearded trees,
Full-skirted dancers risen from a dream.

Birds call; twigs crackle; wild marsh grasses sway;
Will you come soon, before the cold winds blow
To swirl the dust and drive the leaves away,
And thin-ribbed earth pokes out against the snow?

—WILLIAM JAY SMITH

BEGINNINGS:
Questions, Rhymes, and Riddles

THE SIX BADGERS

As I was a-hoeing, a-hoeing my lands
Six badgers came up with white wands in their hands
They made a ring around me and, bowing, they said:
"Hurry home, Farmer George, for the table is spread!
There's pie in the oven, there's beef on the plate:
Hurry home, Farmer George, if you would not be late!"
So homeward I went, but could not understand
Why six fine dog-badgers with white wands in hand
Should seek me out hoeing and bow in a ring,
And all to inform me so common a thing!

—ROBERT GRAVES

RHYME OF RAIN

"Fifty stories more to fall,
Nothing in our way at all,"
Said a raindrop to its mate,
Falling near the Empire State.
Said the second, "Here we go!
That's Fifth Avenue below."
Said the first one, "There's a hat.
Watch me land myself on that.
Forty stories isn't far—
Thirty-seven—here we are—
Twenty, sixteen, thirteen, ten—"
"If we make this trip again,"
Said the second, "we must fall
Near a building twice as tall."
"What a time to think of that,"
Said the first, and missed the hat.

—JOHN HOLMES

SNOW

I come more softly than a bird,
And lovely as a flower;
I sometimes last from year to year
And sometimes but an hour.

I stop the swiftest railroad train
Or break the stoutest tree.
And yet I am afraid of fire
And children play with me.

—MARY AUSTIN

LADYBIRD

Tiniest of turtles!
Your shining back
Is a shell of orange
With spots of black.

How trustingly you walk
Across this land
Of hairgrass and hollows
That is my hand.

Your small wire legs,
So frail, so thin,
Their touch is swansdown
Upon my skin.

There! break out
Your wings and fly
No tenderer creature
Beneath the sky.

—CLIVE SANSOM

MY VALENTINE

I will make you brooches
And toys for your delight
Of bird song at morning
And starshine at night.
I will build a palace
Fit for you and me,

Of green days in forests
And blue days at sea.

—ROBERT LOUIS STEVENSON

THE CANAL BANK

I know a girl,
And a girl knows me,
And the owl says, what!
And the owl says, who?

But what we know
We both agree
That nobody else
Shall hear or see;

It's all between herself and me:
To wit? said the owl,
To woo! said I,
To-what! To-wit! To-woo!

—JAMES STEPHENS

THE SONG OF THE MISCHIEVOUS DOG

There are many who say that a dog has its day,
    And a cat has a number of lives;
There are others who think that a lobster is pink,
    And that bees never work in their hives.
There are fewer, of course, who insist that a horse
    Has a horn and two humps on its head,
And a fellow who jests that a mare can build nests
    Is as rare as a donkey that's red.
Yet in spite of all this, I have moments of bliss,
    For I cherish a passion for bones,
And though doubtful of biscuit, I'm willing to risk it,
    And love to chase rabbits and stones.
But my greatest delight is to take a good bite
    At a calf that is plump and delicious;
And if I indulge in a bite at a bulge,
    Let's hope you won't think me too vicious.

—DYLAN THOMAS

(written in 1925 when Dylan was eleven years old)

WHEN DID THE WORLD BEGIN

"When did the World begin and how?"
I asked a lamb, a goat, a cow:

"What's it all about and why?"
I asked a hog as he walked by:

"Where will the whole thing end, and when?"
I asked a duck, a goose, a hen:

And I copied all the answers too,
A quack, a honk, an oink, a moo.

—ROBERT CLAIRMONT

THE CLOCK

Here's what I think
about a clock:
it should be tired
ticktocking all the time—
tight-wired,
wheels whizzing,
dizzying,
hands creeping,
never sleeping.

Well, I've had it all apart
and back again,
even the main-
spring,
sort of testing
it. And now
I've fixed it somehow
so the clock is
resting.

—FELICE HOLMAN

MISS T.

It's a very odd thing—
    As odd as can be—
That whatever Miss T. eats
    Turns into Miss T.;
Porridge and apples,
    Mince, muffins, and mutton,
Jam, junket, jumbles—
    Not a rap, not a button
It matters; the moment
    They're out of her plate,
Though shared by Miss Butcher
    And sour Mr. Bate,
Tiny and cheerful,
    And neat as can be,
Whatever Miss T. eats
    Turns into Miss T.

—WALTER DE LA MARE

THE LONELY SCARECROW

My poor old bones—I've only two—
A broomshank and a broken stave.
My ragged gloves are a disgrace.
My one peg-foot is in the grave.

I wear the labourer's old clothes:
Coat, shirt, and trousers all undone.
I bear my cross upon a hill
In rain and shine, in snow and sun.

I cannot help the way I look.
My funny hat is full of hay.
—O, wild birds, come and nest in me!
Why do you always fly away?

—JAMES KIRKUP

BUNCHES OF GRAPES

"Bunches of grapes," says Timothy
   "Pomegranates pink," says Elaine;
"A junket of cream and a cranberry tart
   For me," says Jane.

"Love-in-a-mist," says Timothy;
   "Primroses pale," says Elaine;
"A nosegay of pinks and mignonette
   For me," says Jane.

"Chariots of gold," says Timothy;
   "Silvery wings," says Elaine;
"A bumpity ride in a wagon of hay
   For me," says Jane.

—WALTER DE LA MARE

THE TOASTER

A silver-scaled Dragon with jaws flaming red
Sits at my elbow and toasts my bread.
I hand him fat slices, and then, one by one,
He hands them back when he sees they are done.

—WILLIAM JAY SMITH

CONVERSATION

"Mother, may I stay up tonight?"
"No, dear."
"Oh dear! (She always says 'No, dear.')
But Father said I might."
"No, dear."
"He did, that is, if you thought it right."
"No, dear, it isn't right."
"Oh dear! Can I keep on the light?"
"No, dear. In spite
Of what your Father said,
You go to bed,
And in the morning you'll be bright
And glad instead
For one more day ahead."
"I might,
But not for one more night."
"No, dear—*no*, dear."
"At least I've been polite, I guess."
"Yes, dear, you've been polite—
Good night."
"Oh dear,
I'd rather stay down here—
I'm quite . . ."
"No, dear. Now, out of sight."
("Well that was pretty near—")
"*Good* night."
("—all right.")
"Good *night!*"

—DAVID MCCORD

EARLY SUPPER

Laughter of children brings
 The kitchen down with laughter.
While the old kettle sings
Laughter of children brings
To a boil all savory things.
 Higher than beam or rafter,
Laughter of children brings
 The kitchen down with laughter.

So ends an autumn day,
 Light ripples on the ceiling,
Dishes are stacked away;
So ends an autumn day,
The children jog and sway
 In comic dances wheeling.
So ends an autumn day,
 Light ripples on the ceiling.

They trail upstairs to bed,
 And night is a dark tower.
The kettle calls: instead
They trail upstairs to bed,
Leaving warmth, the coppery-red
 Mood of their carnival hour.
They trail upstairs to bed,
 And night is a dark tower.

—BARBARA HOWES

WILL YOU COME?

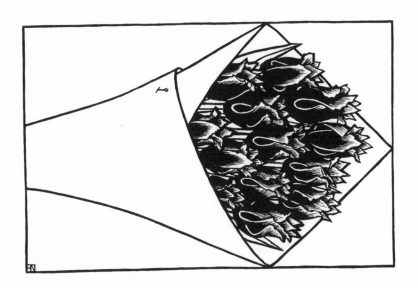

GO HOME

to the fence posts leaning,
the drive pocked.
See the barns stained brown, tobacco red,
their slatted sides tattooed:
Big Chief, Happy Jim.

Drive down the pale macadam road;
pass the Burcold farm
where all the blue-eyed Burcolds live
displaying kinship like a deck of cards.

Wave to the barley.
Wave to the white cows spotted
dark under the willows.

Listen, listen to the thin tar patches
bump under the tires:
welcome home; welcome home.

—JANET REED MCFATTER

WILL YOU COME?

Will you come?
Will you come?
Will you ride
So late
At my side?
O, will you come?

Will you come?
Will you come
If the night
Has a moon,
Full and bright?
O, will you come?

Would you come?
Would you come
If the noon
Gave light,
Not the moon?
Beautiful, would you come?

Would you have come?
Would you have come
Without scorning,
Had it been
Still morning?
Beloved, would you have come?

If you come
Haste and come.
Owls have cried;
It grows dark
To ride.
Beloved, beautiful, come.

—EDWARD THOMAS

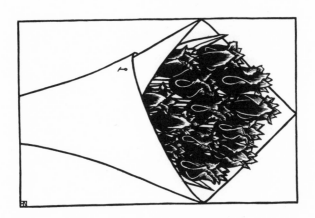

THE QUEEN OF THE NILE

Said the Queen of the Nile
　By the green palm tree:
　　"It is Our desire
　　　That you come to tea
　　　　Thursday at twenty-three
　　　　Past three
　　　　　Under the Royal Canopy
　　　　　In Our Golden Barge
　　　　　On the River Nile
　　　　　　Beside the Mediterranean
　　　　　　Sea."

I bowed, and said:
　"Most certainly!"
　　To the Queen of the Nile
　　By the green palm tree.

—WILLIAM JAY SMITH

AFTERNOON ON A HILL

I will be the gladdest thing
    Under the sun!
I will touch a hundred flowers
    And not pick one.

I will look at cliffs and clouds
    With quiet eyes,
Watch the wind bow down the grass,
    And the grass rise.

And when lights begin to show
    Up from the town,
I will mark which must be mine,
    And then start down!

—EDNA ST. VINCENT MILLAY

VISIT

It is not far to my place:
you can come smallboat,
pausing under shade in the eddies
    or going ashore
        to rest, regard the leaves

    or talk with birds and
shore weeds: hire a full-grown man not
late in years to oar you
    and choose a canoe-like thin ship;
        (a dumb man is better and no

    costlier; he will attract
the reflections and silences under leaves:)
travel light: a single book, some twine:
    the river is muscled at rapids with trout
        and a laurel limb

    will make a suitable spit: if you
leave in the forenoon, you will arrive
with plenty of light
    the afternoon of the third day: I will
        come down to the landing

(tell your man to look for it,
the dumb have clear sight and are free of
visions) to greet you with some made
    wine and a special verse:
        or you can come by shore:

        choose the right: there the rocks
cascade less frequently, the grade more gradual:
treat yourself gently: the ascent thins both
    mind and blood and you must
        keep still a dense reserve

        of silence we can poise against
conversation: there is little news:
I found last month a root with shape and
    have heard a new sound among
        the insects: come.

—A. R. AMMONS

THE LAST WORD OF A BLUEBIRD

As Told to a Child

As I went out a Crow
In a low voice said "Oh,
I was looking for you.
How do you do?
I just came to tell you
To tell Lesley (will you?)
That her little Bluebird
Wanted me to bring word
That the north wind last night
That made the stars bright
And made ice on the trough
Almost made him cough
His tail feathers off.
He just had to fly!
But he sent her Good-by,
And said to be good,
And wear her red hood,
And look for skunk tracks
In the snow with an ax—
And do everything!
And perhaps in the spring
He would come back and sing."

—ROBERT FROST

THE GOOSE
IN THE BOTTLE
Poems About Poetry

POETRY DEFINED

That day everything went wrong.
Too hot to be too sticky.
It wasn't dignified, like fate,
Or awkward, like unlucky.
It was a day so contrary
From failed morning to wasted night
That several things that always
Went wrong went right.
The limit was a live goose
I had put in a big bottle,
Not thinking what I was about,
Till someone asked me how
With no glassbreak or bloodshed
Ever I could get it out.
"There it is!" I yelled. "There!"
Said they, "There where?"
"Not in the bottle now,
And no breakage either. How?
I put it in with my words.
I took it out the same way.
And what worked with these
Can with any words, I say."

—JOHN HOLMES

TO AN ARTIST, TO TAKE HEART

Slipping in blood, by his own hand, through pride,
Hamlet, Othello, Coriolanus fall.
Upon his bed, however, Shakespeare died,
Having endured them all.

—LOUISE BOGAN

THE STROLLING PLAYER

My hands in pockets worn out at the seams,
And clad in a coat that was almost perfect, too,
I traveled, Muse, and I was true to you;
How splendid were the loves I found in dreams!

I had a large hole in my pants, my only pair.
Like Tom Thumb, dreamer lad, I formed my rhymes;
I stayed at the Sign of the Dipper several times.
My stars made a sound like silk in the high, night air.

I'd hear them on the highway when I stopped
Those good September evenings while dew dropped,
Cooling my head like wine poured in the dark;

When rhyming in those shadowed, eerie places,
Like lyre strings I'd pluck the elastic laces
Of my battered shoes, one foot against my heart.

—ARTHUR RIMBAUD

(translated from the French by William Jay Smith)

I SPEAK, I SAY, I TALK

Cats purr.
Lions roar.
Owls hoot.
Bears snore.
Crickets creak.
Mice squeak.
Sheep baa.
But I SPEAK!

Monkeys chatter.
Cows moo.
Ducks quack.
Doves coo.
Pigs squeal.
Horses neigh.
Chickens cluck.
But I SAY!

Flies hum.
Dogs growl.
Bats screech.
Coyotes howl.
Frogs croak.
Parrots squawk.
Bees buzz.
But I TALK!

—ARNOLD L. SHAPIRO

A CAPPELLA

Backed correctly into a corner,
the scrolled old upright

is the piano my landlord left,
having no better place
than my quiet quarters

for a large, homely, worn,
quite worthless music box.

I don't play. Save to
an imagination that prefers
things to be as they should,

there's no loss in the dead
keys up and down the board,

like pickets missing
from a fence, or gaps
in a once measured memory.

I use its different levels,
its mute wooden ledges,

to store an odd assembly
of the most ordinary things,
my own a cappella score:

the expensive thin volumes,
a winter-bitten ball glove,

a green growing thing,
my stained straw hat,
a glass, cigarettes, ashes—

why the poor piano's trashed
with all my bit pieces.

I can't play, and I want
what that strong silent type
has somewhere inside—

blues, jazz, swing,
boogie-woogie, ragtime!

—MICHAEL PETTIT

RAINBOW WRITING

Nasturtiums with
their orange cries
flare like trumpets;
their music dies.

Golden harps
of butterflies;
the strings are mute
in autumn skies.

Vermilion chords,
then silent gray;
the last notes of
the song of day.

Rainbow colors
fade from sight,
come back to me
when I write.

—EVE MERRIAM

EATING POETRY

Ink runs from the corners of my mouth.
There is no happiness like mine.
I have been eating poetry.

The librarian does not believe what she sees.
Her eyes are sad
and she walks with her hands in her dress.

The poems are gone.
The light is dim.
The dogs are on the basement stairs and coming up.

Their eyeballs roll,
their blond legs burn like brush.
The poor librarian begins to stamp her feet and weep.

She does not understand.
When I get on my knees and lick her hand,
she screams.

I am a new man.
I snarl at her and bark.
I romp with joy in the bookish dark.

—MARK STRAND

POEM CALLED POEM

This poem is written in an ancient form—
This poem is old and good for walking with
In a city where girls get robbed to learn
The underground, and how to catch their breath

And go on breathing with a small gun on them.
This poem is loaded, shoots to hurt, not kill,
It is a kind of dope, a little sin
Meant to disarm a woman of her will—

Protects you from the fiends but not from me,
Which is the point of any poem's aim.
I'm in this poem. I am a bad shot, Sweet,
But often, like a Gatling gun. Mean mean

Mean. I will give you kisses again next time
In a safe place. This poem is an ancient form.

—JAMES WHITEHEAD

WILD HORSE

I have struggled all day with a thought like a wild noble horse
To make it tread to the measure of a verse;

Now I give over— Tamed, what should it be, after all
But a beast of burden, or a sight for the carnival?

Let it go, let it run free, to be seen only by those who can follow
    in its perilous track,
Or if it must be ridden at last, let it bear a hero on its back.

—ELDER OLSON

ABOUT MOTION PICTURES

"Get the verb right
          and directing is a cinch,"
he said modestly, gesturing
toward his newest masterpiece.

The same is said for poetry.
Strike adjectives, adverbs!
Red-pencil ands and buts.
Get the verb right
          and writing is a cinch.

It's true in living.
          Move. Scintillate.
          Grasp. Dodge.
                    Placate.
                         Glow.
Get the verb right
          and living is a cinch.

The verb is get.

—ANN DARR

MERCE CUNNINGHAM AND THE BIRDS

Last night I saw Merce Cunningham and his ten amazing
dancers dancing for eighty minutes without a break in the
college gym.

      I am trying to tell you how it was
                but of course there are no words
                for being wholly enclosed in a space,
            a tight cocoon without chinks
            so none of the wonder will leak out.

      Instead, I ask you to watch the assorted birds
      feeding outside this window,
      darting and dropping and zeroing in,
      assuming positions in groups of threes
                or fours, to break up and form
                new patterns, other groups

      how each incessant performer
      signals a personal flash of color:
      cardinal red, jay blue,
      towhee orange, March pea green
                of not-yet-yellow goldfinch,
      always tempered with black

how even their silences prefigure
shifts already known to the muscles

and how none leads or follows
how each moves
to the authority of its brain
its autonomous body

perpetual proof that the world
is energy, that to land
in a certain space at a certain time
is being alive. Watch how they manage
to keep it up till each soul is fed
and then disappear into nowhere.

—LISEL MUELLER

FIRST SONG

Then it was dusk in Illinois, the small boy
After an afternoon of carting dung
Hung on the rail fence, a sapped thing
Weary to crying. Dark was growing tall
And he began to hear the pond frogs all
Calling upon his ear with what seemed their joy.

Soon their sound was pleasant for a boy
Listening in the smoky dusk and the nightfall
Of Illinois, and then from the field two small
Boys came bearing cornstalk violins
And rubbed three cornstalk bows with resins,
And they set fiddling with them as with joy.

It was now fine music the frogs and the boys
Did in the towering Illinois twilight make
And into dark in spite of a right arm's ache
A boy's hunched body loved out of a stalk
The first song of his happiness, and the song woke
His heart to the darkness and into the sadness of joy.

—GALWAY KINNELL

PERSIMMONS AND PLUMS

Words
across
cole slaw
and
salami
fall
into
the mustard
coming out
bitter
and
yellow
and a
knobby-kneed
brownie-headed
knicker wearer
eats them up
savoring some
sweet flavor
he's never tasted before.

—ELIZABETH HODGES

JAPANESE FAN

Painted with one fish, a cucumber,
Two loquats or an ancient poem,
You are both book and signature
Whose leaves I close and open
On seal stamped vermilion, a name.

Membrane folded upon yourself,
Flexing in easy joints
The scents of musk and autumn.

You both reveal and hide
Sympathy and shock.
Open or closed, you are
The eyes of the East,
The paper windows of a soul.

—JAMES KIRKUP

THE ACT OF GUESSING

THE BOTTLE

I have in my hand here a brown bottle.
Guess what's inside.
It's not an imp, or a devil, or a magical porter
Who will carry you and your chattels away from Isfahan.
It's not a poison to remove the king like a blot,
Or a bomb to blow the president out of his chair.
It's not even nothing,
Or a dust-filled syrup with the properties of gall and eglantine,
Or a droplet of the blood of St. Mercurius the Alchemist.
It's not even Coca-Cola.
It's not anything at all.
It's simply what it is.
Here, drink it.
The cork is old and thin.
The liquid itself runs smoothly from the lip.
The fragrance reminds one of a dead brick.
The texture is like rain lying in a puddle of blood.
The taste is a mixture of old iron and crows' tears compounded
    of straw and sticks.
It changes you
Into something different
From what you were before.
Actually it's plain water.
It's the act of guessing that changes you.
And it stings on the way down.

—AL LEVINE

SEUMAS BEG

A man was sitting underneath a tree
Outside the village; and he asked me what
Name was upon this place; and said that he
Was never here before—He told a lot

Of stories to me too. His nose was flat!
I asked him how it happened, and he said
—The first mate of the Holy Ghost did that
With a marling-spike one day; but he was dead,

And jolly good job too; and he'd have gone
A long way to have killed him—Oh, he had
A gold ring in one ear; the other one
—"Was bit off by a crocodile, bedad!"—

That's what he said. He taught me how to chew!
He was a real nice man! He liked me too!

—JAMES STEPHENS

THE SHEPHERD'S HUT

The smear of blue peat smoke
That staggered on the wind and broke,
The only sign of life,
Where was the shepherd's wife,
Who left those flapping clothes to dry,
Taking no thought for her family?
For, as they bellied out
And limbs took shape and waved about,
I thought, She little knows
That ghosts are trying on her children's clothes.

—ANDREW YOUNG

BEING A GIANT

It is hard
being a giant
in a place where there are few giants
and all of them crazy.
The loneliness is the worst part.
If he catches a glimpse
of the bodies of the little people
running in the fields below
it is all he can do
to keep from crying.
On white hot days
he wanders in the hills
eating cattle and young trees
ignoring the sharp pains in his belly.
He carries a small pocket mirror
in which he sometimes
looks at pieces
of his enormous face
and sometimes holds it out
flashing the commandments of the sun
to the empty hills.

—ROBERT MEZEY

CONVERSATION PIECE

By moonlight
At midnight,
Under the vines,
A hotel chair
Settles down moodily before the headlines
Of a still-folded evening newspaper.

The other chair
Of the pair
Lies on its back,
Stiff as in pain,
Having been overturned with an angry crack;
And there till morning, alas, it must remain.

On the terrace
No blood-trace,
No sorry glitter
Of a knife, nothing:
Not even the fine-torn fragments of a letter
Or the dull gleam of a flung-off wedding-ring.

Still stable
On the table
Two long-stemmed glasses,
One full of drink,
Watch how the rat among the vines passes
And how the moon trembles on the crag's brink.

—ROBERT GRAVES

THE WALL OF CHINA

Who ever had
Such a whale of a plan
As the Emperor
Chin Shih Huan?

To build a wall
As long as the land,
And as high as a hill
Was what he planned.

The wall he built
Was straight and bent,
Camels and elephants
On top of it went.

But the steps so narrow
Three would pack—
That was to keep
The Tartars back.

Not many Tartars
With bow and arrow
The steps could mount
That were so narrow.

—PADRAIC COLUM

THE DAISY

Having so rich a treasury, so fine a hoard
Of beauty water-bright before my eyes,
I plucked the daisy only, simple and white
In its fringed frock and brooch of innocent gold.

So is all equilibrium restored:
I leave the noontide wealth of richer bloom
To the destroyer, the impatient ravisher;
The intemperate bee, the immoderate bird.

Of all this beauty felt and seen and heard
I can be frugal and devout and plain,
Deprived so long of light and air and grass,
The shyest flower is sweetest to uncover.

How poor I was: and yet no richer lover
Discovered joy so deep in earth and water;
And in the air that fades from blue to pearl,
And in a flower white-frocked like my small daughter.

—MARYA ZATURENSKA

THE SLEEPING GIANT

(A hill, so named, in Hamden, Connecticut)

The whole day long, under the walking sun
That poised an eye on me from its high floor,
Holding my toy beside the clapboard house
I looked for him, the summer I was four.

I was afraid the waking arm would break
From the loose earth and rub against his eyes
A fist of trees, and the whole country tremble
In the exultant labor of his rise;

Then he with giant steps in the small streets
Would stagger, cutting off the sky, to seize
The roofs from house and home because we had
Covered his shape with dirt and planted trees;

And then kneel down and rip with fingernails
A trench to pour the enemy Atlantic
Into our basin, and the water rush,
With the streets full and all the voices frantic.

That was the summer I expected him.
Later the high and watchful sun instead
Walked low behind the house, and school began,
And winter pulled a sheet over his head.

—DONALD HALL

THE CENTAUR

The summer that I was ten—
Can it be there was only one
summer that I was ten? It must

have been a long one then—
each day I'd go out to choose
a fresh horse from my stable

which was a willow grove
down by the old canal.
I'd go on my two bare feet.

But when, with my brother's jackknife,
I had cut me a long limber horse
with a good thick knob for a head,

and peeled him slick and clean
except a few leaves for the tail,
and cinched my brother's belt

around his head for a rein,
I'd straddle and canter him fast
up the grass bank to the path,

trot along in the lovely dust
that talcumed over his hoofs,
hiding my toes, and turning

his feet to swift half-moons.
The willow knob with the strap
jouncing between my thighs

was the pommel and yet the poll
of my nickering pony's head.
My head and my neck were mine,

yet they were shaped like a horse.
My hair flopped to the side
like the mane of a horse in the wind.

My forelock swung in my eyes,
my neck arched and I snorted.
I shied and skittered and reared,

stopped and raised my knees,
pawed at the ground and quivered.
My teeth bared as we wheeled

and swished through the dust again.
I was the horse and the rider,
and the leather I slapped to his rump

spanked my own behind.
Doubled, my two hoofs beat
a gallop along the bank,

the wind twanged in my mane,
my mouth squared to the bit.
And yet I sat on my steed

quiet, negligent riding,
my toes standing the stirrups,
my thighs hugging his ribs.

At a walk we drew up to the porch.
I tethered him to a paling.
Dismounting, I smoothed my skirt

and entered the dusky hall.
My feet on the clean linoleum
left ghostly toes in the hall.

Where have you been? said my mother.
Been riding, I said from the sink,
and filled me a glass of water.

What's that in your pocket? she said.
Just my knife. It weighted my pocket
and stretched my dress awry.

Go tie back your hair, said my mother.
and *Why is your mouth all green?*
*Rob Roy, he pulled some clover
as we crossed the field,* I told her.

—MAY SWENSON

DIGGING FOR CHINA

"Far enough down is China," somebody said.
"Dig deep enough and you might see the sky
As clear as at the bottom of a well.
Except it would be real—a different sky.
Then you could burrow down until you came
To China! Oh, it's nothing like New Jersey.
There's people, trees, and houses, and all that,
But much, much different. Nothing looks the same."

I went and got the trowel out of the shed
And sweated like a coolie all that morning,
Digging a hole beside the lilac-bush,
Down on my hands and knees. It was a sort
Of praying, I suspect. I watched my hand
Dig deep and darker, and I tried and tried
To dream a place where nothing was the same.
The trowel never did break through to blue.

Before the dream could weary of itself
My eyes were tired of looking into darkness,
My sunbaked head of hanging down a hole.
I stood up in a place I had forgotten,
Blinking and staggering while the earth went round
And showed me silver barns, the fields dozing
In palls of brightness, patens growing and gone
In the tides of leaves, and the whole sky china blue.
Until I got my balance back again
All that I saw was China, China, China.

—RICHARD WILBUR

IN GOOD RELATION
TO THE EARTH

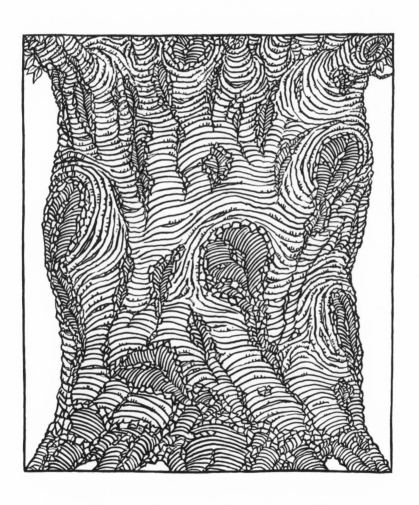

THE DELIGHT SONG OF TSOAI-TALEE

I am a feather in the bright sky.
I am the blue horse that runs in the plain.
I am the fish that rolls, shining, in the water.
I am the shadow that follows a child.
I am the evening light, the lustre of meadows.
I am an eagle playing with the wind.
I am a cluster of bright beads.
I am the farthest star.
I am the cold of the dawn.
I am the roaring of the rain.
I am the glitter on the crust of the snow.
I am the long track of the moon in a lake.
I am a flame of four colors.
I am a deer standing away in the dusk.
I am a field of sumac and the pomme blanche.
I am an angle of geese upon the winter sky.
I am the hunger of a young wolf.
I am the whole dream of these things.

You see, I am alive, I am alive.
I stand in good relation to the earth.
I stand in good relation to the gods.
I stand in good relation to all that is beautiful.
I stand in good relation to the daughter of Tsen-tainte.
You see, I am alive, I am alive.

—N. SCOTT MOMADAY

THE RED WHEELBARROW

so much depends
upon

a red wheel
barrow

glazed with rain
water

beside the white
chickens

—WILLIAM CARLOS WILLIAMS

SIMULTANEOUSLY

Simultaneously, five thousand miles apart,
two telephone poles, shaking and roaring
and hissing gas, rose from their emplacements
straight up, leveled off and headed
for each other's land, alerted radar
and ground defense, passed each other
in midair, escorted by worried planes,
and plunged into each other's place,
steaming and silent and standing straight,
sprouting leaves.

—DAVID IGNATOW

THE DANCE

In Breughel's great picture, The Kermess,
the dancers go round, they go round and
around, the squeal and the blare and the
tweedle of bagpipes, a bugle and fiddles
tipping their bellies (round as the thick-
sided glasses whose wash they impound)
their hips and their bellies off balance
to turn them. Kicking and rolling about
the Fair Grounds, swinging their butts, those
shanks must be sound to bear up under such
rollicking measures, prance as they dance
in Breughel's great picture, The Kermess.

—WILLIAM CARLOS WILLIAMS

COUNTRY STARS

The nearsighted child has taken off her glasses
and come downstairs to be kissed goodnight.
She blows on a black windowpane until it's white.
Over the apple trees a great bear passes
but she puts her own construction on the night.

Two cities, a chemical plant, and clotted cars
breathe our distrust of darkness on the air,
clouding the pane between us and the stars.
But have no fear, or only proper fear:
the bright watchers are still there.

—WILLIAM MEREDITH

OLD MAN, THE SWEAT LODGE

"This small lodge is now
The womb of our mother, Earth.
This blackness in which we sit,
The ignorance of our impure minds.
These burning stones are
The coming of new life."
I keep his words near my heart.

Confessing, I recall my evil deeds.
For each sin, I sprinkle water on fire-hot stones;
The hissing steam is sign that
The place from which Earth's seeds grow
Is still alive.
He sweats.
I sweat.

I remember, Old Man heals the sick,
Brings good fortune to one deserving.
Sacred steam rises;
I feel my pores give out their dross.
After I chant prayers to the Great Spirit,
I raise the door to the East.
Through this door dawns wisdom.

Cleansed, I dive into icy waters.
Pure, I wash away all of yesterday.
"My son, walk in this new life.
It is given to you.
Think right, feel right.
Be happy."
I thank you, Old Man, the Sweat Lodge.

—PHIL GEORGE

MAGPIE

Eight-toes, teetering
    Sabre unscabbarded,
      Bellying spinnaker

Fast to a fencepost,
    Gape your black bill
      In a squawk clean as kindling!

On, with a smother
    Of saw-toothed wingbeats,
      My piebald jolly-boat!

Surge hull down
    Past the crest of the ridge
      Where the wind breaks, breaks
      All day like foam.

——PETER DAVISON

THE STORY OF A WELL-MADE SHIELD

Now in the dawn before it dies, the eagle swings low
and wide in a great arc, curving downward to the place
of origin. There is no wind, but there is a long roaring
on the air. It is like the wind—nor is it quite like the
wind—but more powerful.

——N. SCOTT MOMADAY

FAMILY

When you swim in the surf off Seal Rocks, and your family
Sits in the sand
Eating potato salad, and the undertow
Comes which takes you out away down
To loss of breath loss of play and the power of play
Holler, say
Help, help, help. Hello, they will say,
Come back here for some potato salad.

It is then that a seventeen-year-old cub
Cruising in a helicopter from Antigua,
A jackstraw expert speaking only Swedish
And remote from this area as a camel, says
Look down there, there is somebody drowning.
And it is you. You say, yes, yes,
And he throws you a line.
This is what is called the brotherhood of man.

—JOSEPHINE MILES

DEER HUNT, SALT LAKE VALLEY

I follow the deer through shadows
at dawn in the foothills, in the cool air of July.
Autumn is on the berries. The sun comes
as sharp and bright as desert bone.
Sagebrush is damp with dew;
and earth flows on all sides like water that has no reality.
We dream and make things true.
I ride over rocks as solid as mountains,
through scrub oak and sweetpea, wild and purple.
Magpies screech overhead,
Shale breaks underfoot.
I follow the deer in July.
I follow the deer.
I want to know how they feel, the deer,
in the canyons
in the lavender haze of shadows carved by dawn—
I want to know how they feel as they come this day from
      the pure, cool shadows
down to the edge, down to the hard, final edge.

—HELEN HANDLEY

GOOD TIMES

LEAVING MENDOTA, 1956

Fat red barns lean east along Highway 109.
Black soft cows float into the willows.
Coons among the cattails bite off the heads of crabs.
Grackles strut and spade for sow bugs.
Healthy rats sing in the bins.
On the ridgepole the running horse spins and spins.

—LAWRENCE LOCKE

GOOD TIMES

My Daddy has paid the rent
and the insurance man is gone
and the lights is back on
and my uncle Brud has hit
for one dollar straight
and they is good times
good times
good times

My Mama has made bread
and Grampaw has come
and everybody is drunk
and dancing in the kitchen
and singing in the kitchen
oh these is good times
good times
good times

oh children think about the
good times

—LUCILLE CLIFTON

CLABE MOTT

Arise from your rope-strung bed, Clabe Mott,
The sun rakes the fields, your farm stands fallow,
The mouldboard rusts, the plowstock stands upturned,
The harness falls in heaps within your sagging barn
And your stock runs free upon the brambled hills.

The beard is thin upon your face, Clabe Mott,
Your hands are slender as a willow's bough.
How could your slim feet plod the furrows down?
How could you hold a mountain in your arms,
Or slay a forest with your papered hand?

Fetch out the fiddle, Clabe, draw the ready bow,
Let crabgrass march, let foxtail drown the patch,
Let dull-chains slacken, the poplars stand unhewn,
Forget the partridge in the fence-row thatch.

When you strike fire on your fiddle, Clabe,
The waters wait, the winds break their pace,
The corn grows tall, the shoat farrows young,
The foals race pasture with the golden mare;
Strong men wait, calloused hands go slack,
The oaks go down with thunder in the singing air.

—JAMES STILL

AFTER THE HURRICANE

After the hurricane, the shallows clogged
with silt and webs of weed against the docks.
An empty gondola bobbed waterlogged
and battered near a piling wet for yards
above the rivermark.

Inland, the grass flashed green beyond belief.
Barberries and branches littered all the lawns
where gales had shaken them, and every leaf
that furled against the whipping flames of wind
unfolded like a flag

to sun and rainbow and the clear wonder
of sky—and more than sky. For I remembered
sabbaths of calm after the blood's thunder
undid the world in rituals of fury
and returned to zero.

—SAMUEL HAZO

LOVE IS

a flock of birds, soaring, twisting, turning,
floating, lifting, swooping, landing, splitting into
pieces (individual birds) that can peck peck peck
before they once again unite in the flock that, rising,
goes reeling, shifting, flying (flying, that's the word
I was looking for) right out of sight.

—ANN DARR

INVIOLABLE

Horse, huge
On the hilltop
Leaning

Massy chest
To the open sky,
Unhaltered sun,

Meadows and
The hankering sea
Embracing—

O great
Creatures I would clasp
And nuzzle

Over the barbed
Wire fence
Though I trespass

My boundaries,
Breaking
Your laws.

—DANIEL HOFFMAN

A BLESSING

Just off the highway to Rochester, Minnesota,
Twilight bounds softly forth on the grass.
And the eyes of those two Indian ponies
Darken with kindness.
They have come gladly out of the willows
To welcome my friend and me.
We step over the barbed wire into the pasture
Where they have been grazing all day, alone.
They ripple tensely, they can hardly contain their happiness
That we have come.
They bow shyly as wet swans. They love each other.
There is no loneliness like theirs.
At home once more,
They begin munching the young tufts of spring in the darkness.
I would like to hold the slenderer one in my arms.
For she has walked over to me
And nuzzled my left hand.
She is black and white,
Her mane falls wild on her forehead,
And the light breeze moves me to caress her long ear
That is delicate as the skin over a girl's wrist.
Suddenly I realize
That if I stepped out of my body I would break
Into blossom.

—JAMES WRIGHT

DANCE ON PUSHBACK

Rein your sorry nags, boys, buckle the polished saddle
And set black hats aslant the wind down Troublesome,
There are doings on Pushback at Gabe Waye's homeplace
And the door hangs wide, the thumping keg bubbles
With gonesome plumping in the elderberry patch;
The cider brew strains against red cob stoppers
And the puncheon floor is mealed for the skip and shuffle,
Ready for the stamping, waiting for the hopping,
The Grapevine swing, the old Virginie reeling
In the grease lamp's fuming and unsteady gleaming.
There are jolly fellows heading toward Pushback
In the valley's brisk breathing, the moon's white bathing,
In the whippoorwill's lonesome never answered calling.

Gabe Waye has six fair young daughters
Who dance like foxfire in dark thickets,
Whose feet are nimble, whose bodies are willowy,
As smooth as yellow poplars in early bud,
And their cheeks are like maple leaves in early autumn,
And their breath as sweet as fresh mountain tea.
Gabe Waye has six full-blooming daughters
With dresses starched as stiff as galax leaves,
Awaiting the dancing, awaiting and hoping.

Rein-up the filly, boys, hitch-up the stallion
And heigh-o yonder toward Pushback Mountain,
The katydids a-calling, the hoot-owl a-hooting,
Thick hoofs are striking fire on the crookedy trail,
For feet are yearning for the heart-leaf weaving
And a sight of Waye's daughters doing the Fare-you-well.

Gabe Waye has three tall strapping sons
Standing six feet five in wide bare feet,
And with handsome faces where laughter's never fading,
And with swift limber fingers for silver strings twanging.
The tallest picks the banjo, the thickest saws the fiddle,
The broadest plays the dulcimer with the readiest grace,
And the three together set the darkling hollow ringing
While the harmony goes tripping over moon-dappled hill.

Spur-up the nags, boys, the dance won't be lasting,
Tighten up the reins and set the pebbles flying,
Heigh-o to Pushback with a quick lick-a-spittle,
Night will be fading and moonlight dying.

—JAMES STILL

SKYCOAST

I'd build a house with windows
    in the roof so I could see
    from underneath the plunge
    and spatter of rain, snow
    in a bluster, hail hitting . . .
Having a skycoast would
    liven me more than living
    near the sea.
            No sound.
                      No
smell.
       No villainy.
                Air
is my element.
           Its pitch
and pressure keep me
as and what I am.
No one can drown in it.

           —SAMUEL HAZO

MOVING BETWEEN BELOIT AND MONROE

The car conveys us where we've been
because the scene discovers
over and over one simple green
to keep spring's mud and tubules covered.

Because the scene discovers
how grain bean grass and clover stir
to keep spring's mud and tubules covered,
the fields pass for one another.

How grain bean grass and clover stir!
Since newness grows everywhere the same,
the fields pass for one another
this month, murmuring its lovely name.

Since newness grows everywhere the same,
the car seems to stand still over
this month murmuring its lovely name
in permutations like a lover.

The car seems to stand still over—
over and over—one simple green
in permutations. Like a lover
the car conveys us where we've been.

—BINK NOLL

THE FLOOR
AND THE CEILING
Nonsense Poems

THE PICKET FENCE

There used to be a picket fence
with space to gaze from hence to thence.

An architect who saw this sight
approached it suddenly one night,

removed the spaces from the fence,
and built of them a residence.

The picket fence stood there dumbfounded
with pickets wholly unsurrounded,

a view so naked and obscene,
the Senate had to intervene.

The architect, however, flew
to Afri- or Americoo.

—CHRISTIAN MORGENSTERN

(translated from the German by Max Knight)

THE FLOOR AND THE CEILING

Winter and summer, whatever the weather,
The Floor and the Ceiling were happy together
In a quaint little house on the outskirts of town
With the Floor looking up and the Ceiling looking down.

The Floor bought the Ceiling an ostrich-plumed hat,
And they dined upon drippings of bacon fat,
Diced artichoke hearts and cottage cheese
And hundreds of other such delicacies.

On a screened-in porch in early spring
They would sit at the player piano and sing.
When the Floor cried in French, *"Ah, je vous adore!"*
The Ceiling replied, "You adorable Floor!"

The years went by as the years they will,
And each little thing was fine until
One evening, enjoying their bacon fat,
The Floor and the Ceiling had a terrible spat.

The Ceiling, loftily looking down,
Said, "You are the *lowest* Floor in this town!"
The Floor, looking up with a frightening grin,
Said, "Keep up your chatter, and *you* will cave in!"

So they went off to bed: while the Floor settled down,
The Ceiling packed up her gay wallflower gown;
And tiptoeing out past the Chippendale chair
And the gateleg table, down the stair,

Took a coat from the hook and a hat from the rack,
And flew out the door—farewell to the Floor!—
And flew out the door, and was seen no more,
And flew out the door, and *never* came back!

In a quaint little house on the outskirts of town,
Now the shutters go bang, and the walls tumble down;
And the roses in summer run wild through the room,
But blooming for no one—then why should they bloom?

For what is a Floor now that brambles have grown
Over window and woodwork and chimney of stone?
For what is a Floor when the Floor stands alone?
And what is a Ceiling when the Ceiling has flown?

—WILLIAM JAY SMITH

THE SMOKED HERRING

There was a great white wall—bare, bare, bare,
Against the wall a ladder—high, high, high,
And, on the ground, a smoked herring—dry, dry, dry,

He comes, bearing in his hands—so dirty, dirty, dirty,
A heavy hammer, a great nail—sharp, sharp, sharp,
A ball of string—so big, big, big.

Then he climbs the ladder—high, high, high,
And drives the pointed nail—toc, toc, toc,
Into the top of the great white wall—bare, bare, bare.

He lets the hammer go—it falls, falls, falls,
Ties to the nail the string—so long, long, long,
And, to the end, the smoked herring—dry, dry, dry.

He descends the ladder—so high, high, high,
Carries it away, with the hammer—so heavy, heavy, heavy,
And so he goes away—far, far, far.

And ever since the smoked herring—dry, dry, dry,
At the end of the string—so long, long, long,
Very slowly swings—for ever, ever, ever.

I have made up this little tale—so simple, simple, simple,
Just to enrage people—so grave, grave, grave,
And to amuse children—so small, small, small.

—CHARLES CROS

(*translated from the French by A. L. Lloyd*)

THE THREE FOXES

Once upon a time there were three little foxes
Who didn't wear stockings, and they didn't wear sockses,
But they all had handkerchiefs to blow their noses,
And they kept their handkerchiefs in cardboard boxes.

They lived in the forest in three little houses,
And they didn't wear coats, and they didn't wear trousies.
They ran through the woods on their little bare tootsies,
And they played "Touch last" with a family of mouses.

They didn't go shopping in the High Street shopses,
But caught what they wanted in the woods and copses.
They all went fishing, and they caught three wormses,
They went out hunting, and they caught three wopses.

They went to a Fair, and they all won prizes—
Three plum-puddingses and three mince-pieses.
They rode on elephants and swang on swingses,
And hit three coco-nuts at coco-nut shieses.

That's all that I know of the three little foxes
Who kept their handkerchiefs in cardboard boxes.
They lived in the forest in three little houses,
But they didn't wear coats and they didn't wear trousies,
And they didn't wear stockings and they didn't wear sockses.

—A. A. MILNE

FATHER AND MOTHER

My father's name is Frankenstein,
He comes from the Barbados.
He fashioned me from package twine
And instant mashed potatoes.

My mother's name is Draculeen,
She lets a big bat bite her,
And folks who sleep here overnight
Wake up a few quarts lighter.

—X. J. KENNEDY

GREAT-GREAT GRANDMA, DON'T SLEEP IN YOUR TREEHOUSE TONIGHT

Great-great Grandma, don't sleep in your tree-
house tonight,
Don't swing on your rope and your tire,
'Cause your tree felt the bite
Of a mighty termite—
Have a seat
By the heat
Of the fire!

Here's a big bowl of black bolts and nuts you can
crack,
Here's some cider to slide down your craw,
Oh, what fun it'll be
While we roast that old tree—
None so tall
Stands in all
Arkansas!

—X. J. KENNEDY

ELECTRICITY IS FUNNY!

Would Edison get the blues if he blew a fuse?
No! So why cry if your light bulbs die?
Don't get bugged by a plug if it burns up your rug!
Laugh! It's a joke when the wires start to smoke!
No need to frown if the house burns down,
Just take it in stride with remarks that are snide.
For a joke that is rich, cop a look at a switch
Or just for a gag put a bulb in a bag.
Electricity's a riot!

The End

—JOHN CURRIER

THE DONKEY

I had a Donkey, that was all right,
But he always wanted to fly my Kite;
Every time I let him, the string would bust.
Your Donkey is better behaved, I trust.

—THEODORE ROETHKE

THE PURPLE COW

I never saw a Purple Cow,
    I never hope to see one;
But I can tell you, anyhow,
    I'd rather see than be one.

—GELETT BURGESS

SOME SOUND ADVICE FROM SINGAPORE

There was a man from Singapore
Who dressed in everything he wore
And took a walk along the shore.

The shore was right beside the sea.
Mostly—or so it seems to me—
Because of nowhere else to be.

For the same reason as before
The sea was right beside the shore.
As for the man from Singapore

His reason was: If you take care
To dress in everything you wear,
You won't get sunburned walking bare.

—JOHN CIARDI

THE LIZARD

The Time to Tickle a Lizard,
Is Before, or Right After, a Blizzard.
Now the place to begin
Is just under his Chin—
And here's more Advice:
Don't Poke more than Twice
At an Intimate Place like his Gizzard.

—THEODORE ROETHKE

NATURE IN COUPLETS

A Dream of Natural Wonders

Among the birds in the sky above,
I eagerly seek a joint-tailed dove.
In autumn when the flocks are loose,
I scan them all for a lamp-necked goose.
Than win to laurels or crown of myrtle,
I'd rather behold a sweater-necked turtle.
Nothing, I vow, would my life so hallow,
As glimpsing at last a coat-tailed swallow.
By the flower beds the gardener hoses,
My eyes are peeled for glass-colored roses.
And I pray I'll see, looming out of the fog,
Before I die, a book-eared dog.

—CHARLTON OGBURN

MOTHER'S NERVES

My mother said, "If just once more
I hear you slam that old screen door,
I'll tear out my hair! I'll dive in the stove!"
I gave it a bang and in she dove.

—X. J. KENNEDY

TALKING TO ANIMALS

ANIMAL PICTURES

Clumsy in his drunken joints
The Russian Wolfhound
Clambers up the stairs.
Wilting into a sofa,
He becomes a platinum widow,
Filthy rich
And black eyes wickedly bored.

The bull giraffe
Whips back
His bludgeon neck
Like a polo rider
Careening in on
The mallet's crack.

Shaggy sloths hang
By their grapplinghook toes,
Reversing the world
Like bums on benches
Watching the sky.

Like a clutch of startled
Debutantes, the flamingos
Lift a foot and stare.

—LAWRENCE LOCKE

TALKING TO ANIMALS

When there are animals about, who else—
People aside—does one talk to?
They form an environment of ear and eye
Most finely adjusted to turns
Of mood: terror, humor . . .

The domesticated: cats and dogs
Speak freely, handle their own
Lives, adjust our natures
To theirs and back; as cattle—
Those enormous oblongs of good-

Will—did they state their strength,
Could smash a barn a day;
As ducks in their sewing circle
Wonder, wander, flapping their
Fluent tails; as a mare

Lumbers, an iron horse on the turntable,
Setting forth a fact, while her foal's eyes dance
Like legs. Smaller creatures: four
Inches of chipmunk tell hazard
From ruin as people can't . . .

Making oneself understood
To animals—as to people—
Is a question of tone of voice,
Of communication just
Right for that neighbor;

Perhaps of being inside
A hogan, or in the middle
Of anywhere, one's antennae out,
Like my Beaver-Spirit who takes—deep
In his Eskimo ear—much wisdom from a Loon.

—BARBARA HOWES

APARTMENT CATS

The Girls wake, stretch, and pad up to the door.
    They rub my leg and purr:
    One sniffs around my shoe,
    Rich with an outside smell,
    The other rolls back on the floor—
White bib exposed, and stomach of soft fur.

Now, more awake, they re-enact Ben Hur
    Along the corridor,
    Wheel, gallop; as they do,
    Their noses twitching still,
    Their eyes get wild, their bodies tense,
Their usual prudence seemingly withdraws.

And then they wrestle: parry, lock of paws,
    Blind hug of close defense,
    Tail-thump, and smothered mew.
    If either, though, feel claws,
    She abruptly rises, knowing well
How to stalk off in wise indifference.

—THOM GUNN

DENISE

Come here, Denise!
Come let us find a little patch of sun
And meditate a measurement of time.

I have outlived five dogs:
Hector and Hercules,
Genghis the golden,
The fashionable Pamplemousse,
And, lately, Hans of Weimar,
Hans of the amber eyes.

You are my last, Denise;
Life is but one dog more,
Denise, my raisin-bread Dalmatian,
Denise of the delicate crossed paws.

—ROBERT BEVERLY HALE

COW

Your hulk is like some
walnut dresser
standing in the corner of an attic
too huge to move and so becomes
part of the place
in which it stands.

Your flat broad head
is hard and heavy.
Your sandpaper tongue
will wear away
the concrete before your stanchion.

Your violet eyes,
the gaping black pupils
lack the luster
of any difference
in the patterns of your brain.

Somewhere in the caverns of your sides
you carried a calf.
We found her today
wobbling like a wicker basket
in the breeze.

—JANET REED MCFATTER

SEAL

See how he dives
From the rocks with a zoom!
See how he darts
Through his watery room
Past crabs and eels
And green seaweed,
Past fluffs of sandy
Minnow feed!
See how he swims
With a swerve and a twist,
A flip of the flipper,
A flick of the wrist!
Quicksilver-quick,
Softer than spray,
Down he plunges
And sweeps away;
Before you can think,
Before you can utter
Words like "Dill pickle"
Or "Apple butter,"
Back up he swims
Past Sting Ray and Shark,
Out with a zoom,
A whoop, a bark;
Before you can say
Whatever you wish,
He plops at your side
With a mouthful of fish!

—WILLIAM JAY SMITH

BATS

A bat is born
Naked and blind and pale.
His mother makes a pocket of her tail
And catches him. He clings to her long fur
By his thumbs and toes and teeth.
And then the mother dances through the night
Doubling and looping, soaring, somersaulting—
Her baby hangs on underneath.
All night, in happiness, she hunts and flies.
Her high sharp cries
Like shining needlepoints of sound
Go out into the night and, echoing back,
Tell her what they have touched.
She hears how far it is, how big it is,
Which way it's going:
She lives by hearing.
The mother eats the moths and gnats she catches
In full flight; in full flight
The mother drinks the water of the pond
She skims across. Her baby hangs on tight.
Her baby drinks the milk she makes him
In moonlight or starlight, in mid-air.
Their single shadow, printed on the moon
Or fluttering across the stars,
Whirls on all night; at daybreak
The tired mother flaps home to her rafter.
The others all are there.

They hang themselves up by their toes,
They wrap themselves in their brown wings.
Bunched upside down, they sleep in air.
Their sharp ears, their sharp teeth, their quick sharp faces
Are dull and slow and mild.
All the bright day, as the mother sleeps,
She folds her wings about her sleeping child.

—RANDALL JARRELL

THE GRASSHOPPER

Down
a
deep
well
a
grasshopper
fell.

By kicking about
He thought to get out.
    He might have known better,
    For that got him wetter.
To kick round and round
Is the way to get drowned,
    And drowning is what
    I should tell you he got.

        But
        the
        well
        had
        a
        rope
        that
        dangled
        some
        hope.

And sure as molasses
On one of his passes
    He found the rope handy
    And up he went, *and he*
        it
        up
        and
        it
        up
        and
        it
        up
        and
        it
        up
        went

And hopped away proper
As any grasshopper.

—DAVID MCCORD

HORNED LIZARD

Posing on the sloped rock,
warm eggs buried below,
his tongue waits to expel
its dull, adhesive fury.
He jerks the cricket
quickly from the startled grass:
green wings and legs akimbo
jut from his mouth—
Could it be he used to fly?

What to make of his eye
which can still jet blood
from its scaly corners?
Can anything question such witness?

He lingers.
No one else
is so sure
to lift their legs
before moving them ahead.
His skin is like a garden
that refuses to bloom.
As he backs down from his rock
hear the withdrawing sea,
the sea that fled this hovering vengeance.

—CHARLES MOLESWORTH

VULTURE

The vulture's very like a sack
   Set down and left there drooping.
His crooked neck and creaky back
   Look badly bent from stooping
Down to the ground to eat dead cows
   So they won't go to waste
Thus making up in usefulness
   For what he lacks in taste.

—X. J. KENNEDY

DELICATE MOTHER KANGAROO

Delicate mother kangaroo
Sitting up there rabbit-wise, but huge,
   plumb weighted
And lifting her beautiful slender face, oh!
   so much more gently and finely lined than a
   rabbit's or a hare's,
She watches with insatiable wistfulness.
Untold centuries of watching for something to come,
For a new signal from life, in that silent lost
   land of the South.
Where nothing bites but insects and snakes and the
   sun, small life.
Where no bull roared, no cow ever lowed, no stag
   cried, no leopard screeched, no lion coughed,
   no dog barked,
But all was silent save for parrots occasionally,
   in the haunted blue bush.

—D. H. LAWRENCE

CALIFORNIA QUAIL IN JANUARY

Through a Back Window

The covey struts across the chrome-green roof,
Secure and plump and solemnly aloof,
Some twenty quail deployed in neat array.
Their breasts and underparts of velvet gray
Contrast with polished wingtips, gravely bright
With geometric bars of brown and white.
Cheek-marks and forward jutting plumes of black
Mimic Greek helmets moving to attack.
They reach the nearest corner; there the quail
Who leads the marchers halts and spreads his tail.
He mounts with cautious touch the dirt-brown limb
That scrapes upon the eaves, then tries with prim
And graceless steps the tortuous descent.
The covey follows, dignity unbent.
With nervous, liquid clucks they scold their guide
As down the trunk they flutter, fly, and slide.
Once on the ground, the phalanx recombines,
Advancing rank by rank on shriveled vines
That sudden frost has altered overnight
To sooty brown, a universal blight,
And winter furnishes a feast of seeds
From waxen-skinned tomatoes under weeds.
But this unbroken calm is not to be;
A flock of grackles shakes the maple tree
And rises up, a cloud of dirty brown
And opalescent black. It plunges down
With gritty chirps upon the feeding quail.

The vines explode; legs, wings, and feathers flail
In labored takeoff. Finally, gaining height,
The quail betray in throbbing, bullet flight
Their sometime masquerade as earth-bound things,
And dry leaves churn in whirlwinds from their wings.

—WILL C. JUMPER

A FLOCK OF GUINEA HENS SEEN FROM A CAR

The lute and the pear are your half sisters,
The mackerel moon a full first cousin,
And you were born to appear seemly, even when running on
    guinea legs,
As maiden-formed, as single-minded as raindrops,
Ellipses, small homebodies of great orbits (little knots at the back
    like apron strings),
Perfected, sealed off, engraved like a dozen perfect consciences,
As egglike as the eggs you know best, triumphantly speckled . . .
But fast!
Side-eyed with emancipation, no more lost than a string of pearls
    are lost from one another,
You cross the road in the teeth of Pontiacs
As over a threshold, into waving, gregarious grasses,
Welcome wherever you go—the Guinea Sisters.

Bobbins with the threads of innumerable visits behind you,
As light on your feet
As the daughters of Mr. Barrett of Wimpole Street,
Do you ever wonder where Africa has fled?
Is the strangeness of your origins packed tight in those little
    nutmeg heads, so ceremonious, partly naked?
Is there time to ask each other what became of the family wings?
Do you dream?
Princess of Dapple,
Princess of Moonlight,
Princess of Conch,
Princess of Guinealand,

Though you roost in the care of S. Thomas Truly, Rt. 1
(There went his mailbox flying by),
The whole world knows you've never yet given up the secret of
    where you've hidden your nests.

—EUDORA WELTY

THE BLACKBIRD

In the far corner
close by the swings,
every morning
a blackbird sings.

His bill's so yellow,
his coat's so black,
that he makes a fellow
whistle back.

Ann, my daughter,
thinks that he
sings for us two
especially.

—HUMBERT WOLFE

REINDEER AND ENGINE

The reindeer
fastened to the great round eye
that glares along the
Finnish forest track
runs runs runs runs runs
before that blast of light, will die
but not look back

will not
look back, or aside, or swerve
into the black tall deep
good dark of the forests of winter
runs runs runs runs runs
from that light that thrust through his brain's nerve
its whitehot splinter.

The reindeer
has all the forests of Finland to flee
into, its snowy crows and owlly
hush; but over the icy ties
runs runs runs runs runs
from his white round i-
dée fixe until he dies.

To his west
is wide-as-the-moon, to his right
is deep-as-the-dark, but
lockt to his roaring light
runs runs runs runs runs

the fleeing flagging reindeer
from, into, the cold

wheels'

night.

—JOSEPHINE JACOBSEN

THE BULL

In the olive darkness of the sally-trees
silently moved the air from night to day.
The summer-grass was thick with honey-daisies
where he, a curled god, a red Jupiter,
heavy with power among his women lay.

But summer's bubble-sound of sweet creek-water
dwindles and is silent; the seeding grasses
grow harsh, and wind and frost in the black sallies
roughen the sleek-haired slopes. Seek him out, then,
the angry god betrayed, whose godhead passes,

and down the hillsides drive him from his mob.
What enemy steals his strength—what rival steals
his mastered cows? His thunders powerless,
the red storm of his body shrunk with fear,
runs the great bull, the dogs upon his heels.

—JUDITH WRIGHT

WHAT A WAY TO GO!
The World Here and Now

IN PASSING

Open-backed dumpy junktruck
stacked full of old floor-fans,
unplugged, unsteady, undone,
free-whirling like kids' pinwheels
in a last fresh breeze—
What a way to go!

—GERALD JONAS

TIES

When I faded back to pass
Late in the game, as one
Who has been away some time
Fades back into memory,
My father, who had been nodding
At home by the radio,
Would wake, asking
My mother, who had not
Been listening, "What's the score?"
And she would answer, "Tied,"
While the pass I threw
Hung high in the brilliant air
Beneath the dark, like a star.

—DABNEY STUART

TIME PIECE

Take the back off the watch
and see that universe of small parts,
bobbing and turning,
each doing what it should be doing,
and ignoring you completely.

—WILLIAM COLE

CARAVATI'S JUNKYARD

Dried sinks and hot
iceboxes squat on
the chickweed.
Fireless mantels
gape from a shed.

Doors without houses
lean still and stiff
on Caravati's fence.
Doors without handles
unhinged in the sun
peel to their
usable wood.

Beyond stacks of
bannisters, past
piles of wrought
iron railings,
in an empty rag
weed lot,
one door stands up

closing to Caravati's
Junkyard, opening
on goldenrod,
hinging on air.

—ELIZABETH MORGAN

MR. T. S. ELIOT COOKING PASTA

That crackle is well worth hearing.
He breaks in two the macaroni tubes
so as to make them fit the pot,
then casts them with both hands into the water
above the white electric range.
The water bubbles, seethes, the pasta
sinks to the bottom of the pot.
Mr. Eliot casts a glance
through the wide kitchen window toward the park:
it is raining there, and water
pours down the trunks of trees in substantial quantity,
tousling the lawn into a poison-green
Sargasso Sea.
Which reminds him of the pot.
Just so much contemplation has sufficed
for the rising of the pasta
to the water's surface.
He fishes out the bouncing ropes
with a colander, American-made,
and runs cold water on them from the tap.
"One is obliged to do so, otherwise
they will stick together." So Mr. Eliot writes
to a friend, later that evening.
"Still, the most gripping moment
comes when the macaroni
are broken in two with a dry crackle:
in that, somehow,
one recognizes oneself."

—JÓZSEF TORNAI

(*translated from the Hungarian by Richard Wilbur*)

THE DRIVE

Where were we going that
night in the old gray Buick,
seats large as libraries,
wondrous as carved lions?

You could sit
straight up in those seats
and never reach the top
with your head.

With your hand you could hook
your wrist through the loops
pinned to the in-
sides of the car dome,
loops to swing your elbow
like a hammock.

Were we going to look
at a house?
One of the times
we were going maybe to leave the farm

if we could find
someone to buy the cows
and the John Deere,
someone to take the chickens,
and the root cellar
full of old tires.

Night lay on the roof,
slid off the big engine,
wound itself around the axles
like a window shade.
Father's voice, tired and excited
moved in the tones of a prophet.

And we in the back
listening to the hiss of rain,
pretended we were refugees,
wished we were running
for our lives,
wished we were going
nowhere at all.

—JANET REED MCFATTER

FIRST FLIGHT

I watches me climb
in the cockpit, him fixing
the belt and waving
my hand I see

the prop rev and the plane
cough forward
both wings biting
sudden wind

I on ground invisible
sees me taxi obvious
behind him Wild Pilot
what I doing there & here

particularly when
up high he says
Dan,
he says, Dan boy,

take over I don't feel
too good after all
that Scotch-type rot
last night I'm flying

me at the joystick o
boy how come
those chickens getting bigger chasing
their shadows under stoops

I see it clearly
clearly
STICK BACK!
and we climb

higher than the sun
sinking in a stew of clouds
Well Major anything
for a laugh me say

I says let's bring her down

—DANIEL HOFFMAN

CENTRAL HEATING SYSTEM

I'm woken up
By the central heating system. An engine
Thuds in the cellar. Steam clanks in pipes
With distinct sounds—cymbals banged together.
The snow falls outside
Hushing up the scandal of the dark,
Whitewashing the blackness of the boughs.
But here, in the room, the pipes must make their scene.
Like a long watchdog curled through the whole house,
They bark at the ice-fanged killer
Who leaves no footstep in the night.

(*Storrs, Connecticut*)

—STEPHEN SPENDER

MOVING

Early, up without breakfast
I put on yesterday's socks.
There are no others.
All's been consumed
by the boxes.

For days we scrubbed.
Now the kitchen sink
is white as a skull
and throws back light
like a snail's house.

When we walk
the floors ring
and the walls answer.
We are deprived
of light footsteps.

Our voices too
span the air and
like bits of dust
in daylight
shimmy as they fall.

The doors stand open
awaiting the movers.
There are bedsprings
growing on the lawn.

It is time to go.
Already the spiders are hunched
and spinning new webs.

—JANET REED MCFATTER

FRISBEE

Flanged, all bright colors—red, yellow, blue—the discs
Wheel their parabolas, whirl in ellipse,
Soar, dip, or veer, elusive, elegant.
As for the hand that meets them on their way,
It makes the outfielder who gets the ball
Out by the warning track a blatant lout,
A clumsy oaf; the fruitpicker who reaches
Tiptoe on ladder rung for the highest peach,
Apple, or apricot, on the topmost bough,
Cradling it gently, carefully to basket,
Is a lubberly lummox by comparison
With this deft grace, this ease, this perfect neatness.
Oh, never play this game with ugly clothes on.

—ROLFE HUMPHRIES

OKEECHOBEE

Cottonmouth white faces survey the marshes.
"Drain the swamps," they say, "we need
condominiums, jet-ports, room to spread."
Night is a reptile coiled in the willows.
Bulldozers whir in the dawn.

Herons and gallinules stalk the shallows
proclaiming: *invasion, invasion.*
Deer quiver like the water and are gone.
Huge bass deep in the cattails gorge
on their fry, and everywhere the strong
are holding their own. Survival requires control,
but lost somewhere in space the whooping crane's
final cry is speeding toward a star.

—JOHN ALLISON

NIGHT MAIL

This is the night mail crossing the border
Bringing the cheque and the postal order,
Letters for the rich, letters for the poor,
The shop at the corner, the girl next door.
Pulling up Beattock, a steady climb—
The gradient's against her, but she's on time.
Letters of thanks, letters from banks,
Letters of joy from girl and boy,
Receipted bills and invitations,
To inspect new stock or visit relations,
And applications for situations
And timid lovers' declarations,
And gossip, gossip from all the nations,
News circumstantial, news financial,
Letters with holiday snaps to enlarge in,
Letters with faces scrawled on the margin,
Letters from uncles, cousins and aunts,
Letters to Scotland from the South of France,
Letters of condolence to Highlands and Lowlands,
Written on paper of every hue,
The pink, the violet, the white and the blue,
The chatty, the catty, the boring, the adoring,
The cold and official and the heart's outpouring,
Clever, stupid, short and long,
The typed and the printed and the spelt all wrong.

—W. H. AUDEN

COBB WOULD HAVE CAUGHT IT

In sunburnt parks where Sundays lie,
Or the wide wastes beyond the cities,
Teams in grey deploy through sunlight.

Talk it up, boys, a little practice.

Coming in stubby and fast, the baseman
Gathers a grounder in fat green grass,
Picks it stinging and clipped as wit
Into the leather: a swinging step
Wings it deadeye down to first.
Smack. Oh, attaboy, attyoldboy.

Catcher reverses his cap, pulls down
Sweaty casque, and squats in the dust:
Pitcher rubs new ball on his pants,
Chewing, puts a jet behind him;
Nods past batter, taking his time.
Batter settles, tugs at his cap:
A spinning ball: step and swing to it,
Caught like a cheek before it ducks
By shivery hickory: socko, baby:
Cleats dig into dust. Outfielder,
On his way, looking over shoulder,
Makes it a triple. A long peg home.

Innings and afternoons. Fly lost in sunset.
Throwing arm gone bad. There's your old ball game.
Cool reek of the field. Reek of companions.

—ROBERT FITZGERALD

SOLILOQUY IN A MOTEL

I took off down the town's disaster route
And holed up in this hideout by the trail.
The hiss is fading now of their pursuit;
Let ice sink softly in the plastic pail.
Let air flow cold around this rubber foam.
My only home's a home away from home.

It was a fast break, a wild ride did the trick
To get me here past posses of grim men.
Now free TV reruns a western flick
And bandits act it out for me again:
Those lonesome horsemen who've escaped them all,
Galloping over my carpet wall to wall.

Safe and alone in this delicious gloom,
I know the air conditioner's cheerful hum,
And think of those who hid out in this room
And left no sign that this was where they'd come—
The salesmen, tourists, children, covert lovers.
I find fresh glasses in wax paper covers.

All gone, who once took shoes off on this bed
And felt their cars still rocking at their backs,
Those outlaws on the lam—all of them fled.
Like tethered horses outside mountain shacks,
The getaway cars line up for getaway dawn.
This time tomorrow I'll be gone gone gone.

—WALKER GIBSON

SUNDAY NIGHT IN SANTA ROSA

The carnival is over. The high tents,
the palaces of light, are folded flat
and trucked away. A three time loser yanks
the Wheel of Fortune off the wall. Mice
pick through the garbage by the popcorn stand.
A drunken giant falls asleep beside
the juggler, and the Dog-Faced Boy sneaks off
to join the Serpent Lady for the night.
Wind sweeps ticket stubs along the walk.
The Dead Man loads his coffin on a truck.
Off in a trailer by the parking lot
the radio predicts tomorrow's weather
while a clown stares in a dressing mirror,
takes out a box, and peels away his face.

—DANA GIOIA

A SYMPATHY,
A WELCOME
Poems About People

THE BEAN EATERS

They eat beans mostly, this old yellow pair.
Dinner is a casual affair.
Plain chipware on a plain and creaking wood,
Tin flatware.

Two who are Mostly Good.
Two who have lived their day,
But keep on putting on their clothes
And putting things away.

And remembering . . .
Remembering, with twinklings and twinges,
As they lean over the beans in their rented back room that is full
    of beads and receipts and dolls and cloths, tobacco crumbs,
    vases and fringes.

              —GWENDOLYN BROOKS

JANIE SWECKER AND ME AND
GONE WITH THE WIND

Janie Swecker had to act
like she wasn't half
as smart as she was
because if she rattled off
the facts fast as she could
think of them, Miss Jackson
would sniff and say, "Well,
Janie, if you're that bored
with the history of your state,
why don't you go back
in the corner and sit
by yourself?" and Janie
hated that because back
there she couldn't get by
with sneaking to read those
library books she loved
while Miss Jackson drilled
the rest of us. So she made
herself talk slow and give
a wrong answer now and then,
and we stopped teasing her
after we understood that
if we hadn't got it done
she'd do our homework
for us even though she did
C. H. King's and Leo Spraker's
on a regular basis. Janie
let me borrow her mother's
copy of Gone with the Wind,

got impatient with me
to finish it but finally
I did and after that in class
sometimes we'd look at each
other and know what we knew.
One night I even dreamed
Miss Jackson was marching
through Georgia,
Atlanta was burning,
and I was riding hard
to pull Janie
out of the flames.

—DAVID HUDDLE

ITALIAN WOMAN

If Italy is a boot,
then it is on your foot.
An elegant shoe.
Renaissance ladies,
religious and otherwise,
smile out of your face.
Your hand not forgetting a gesture.
Your mouth touching the ocean—
underneath: centuries of crushed shells,
plus the new.

—DIANE WAKOSKI

BREAKINGS

Long before I first left home, my father
tried to teach me horses, land, and sky,
to show me how his kind of work was done.
I studied how to be my father's son,
but all I learned was, when the wicked die,
they ride combines through barley forever.

Every summer I hated my father
as I drove hot horses through dusty grass;
and so I broke with him, and left the farm
for other work, where unfamiliar weather
broke on my head an unexpected storm
and things I had not studied came to pass.

So nothing changes, nothing stays the same,
and I have returned from a broken home
alone, to ask for a job breaking horses.
I watch a colt on a long line making
tracks in dust, and think of the kinds of breakings
there are, and the kinds of restraining forces.

—HENRY TAYLOR

A SYMPATHY, A WELCOME

Feel for your bad fall how could I fail,
poor Paul, who had it so good.
I can offer you only this world like a knife.
Yet you'll get to know your mother,
and, humorless as you do look, you will laugh,
and *all* the others
will not be fierce to you, and loverhood
will swing your soul like a broken bell
deep in a forsaken wood, poor Paul,
whose wild bad father loves you well.

—JOHN BERRYMAN

AUTUMN SONG ON PERRY STREET

Our soprano is on the wind tonight
our slightly off-coloratura.
She and the smell of vanilla
from the National Biscuit Co.
tell us the weather'll be chiller
and the leaves are due to blow.
Somehow the aria's never quite right,
though the areaways endure her
hour upon hour for weeks,
as the back-yard pump starts up
never to, ever to stop.
"One fine—" "One fine day—" she shrieks,
"One fine day he will come—" (Bravura.)
If her voice didn't carry, he might.

—LLOYD FRANKENBERG

I'LL TELL YOU WHAT A FLAPPER IS

a bosom

that was meant to bloom
like any other bosom
but was bound down
to the bone

rope-tied to a
ribcage

and flogged
with long glass beads

in time

the ropes were loosened
but the flapper
did not
rise

it lies there
still

today

flatter than a ping
pong paddle

I know
because I saw one

two, in fact,
head on
in the Ladies locker room
at Natural Bridge

—ANNE HOBSON FREEMAN

TRAVELLING COMPANIONS

"Who's Who," the Bible, and the checkbook always travel with me anywhere I go.—*Statement of a biographee in an advertisement of Vol. 29 of "Who's Who in America."*

The Bible soothes the harried soul,
The checkbook plays an equal role,
"Who's Who," however, of the three,
Most bolsters the biographee,
Who keeps it by him every minute,
Reminding him that he is in it.

—RICHARD ARMOUR

LEARNING

With an insane
back slap the county
school board paid me seven
thousand dollars
to teach
Willie Jones
to write
"i," "I."
Now Willie can write
"I wished I was a long
way from here."
But my own "I" has started to
shrink up and get
dotted
and so me and Willie
are both
leaving for Baltimore.

—EARL SIMPSON

NARCISSA

Some of the girls are playing jacks.
Some are playing ball.
But small Narcissa is not playing
Anything at all.

Small Narcissa sits upon
A brick in her back yard
And looks at tiger lilies,
And shakes her pigtails hard.

First she is an ancient queen
In pomp and purple veil.
Soon she is a singing wind.
And, next, a nightingale.

How fine to be Narcissa,
A-changing like all that!
While sitting still, as still, as still
As anyone ever sat!

—GWENDOLYN BROOKS

THE WHIPPING

The old woman across the way
    is whipping the boy again
and shouting to the neighborhood
    her goodness and his wrongs.

Wildly he crashes through elephant ears,
    pleads in dusty zinnias,
while she in spite of crippling fat
    pursues and corners him.

She strikes and strikes the shrilly circling
    boy till the stick breaks
in her hand. His tears are rainy weather
    to woundlike memories:

My head gripped in bony vise
    of knees, the writhing struggle
to wrench free, the blows, the fear
    worse than blows that hateful

Words could bring, the face that I
    no longer knew or loved . . .
Well, it is over now, it is over,
    and the boy sobs in his room.

And the woman leans muttering against
    a tree, exhausted, purged—
avenged in part for lifelong hidings
    she has had to bear.

—ROBERT HAYDEN

DREAM ABOUT SUNSETS

First of all her name was changed
from Carole to Marian. You and I and Marian
and your mother were in your father's big car
for the purpose of letting you finally choose.
She was beautiful and had all sorts of exotic
suitcases—unmatched snakeskin luggage
in dark Egyptian colours from her trip to Apis
to see the Bulls. I had only one large,
black suitcase. Both of us wore violet-lensed
glasses. Hers were rectangular; mine were old
fashioned ovals—like the ones in my drawer at home.
You chose her. She kept saying how she loved you.
I was speechless and could not answer. I knew
I should say something but was silent.
Then we looked at the most beautiful sunset.
You commented: *Most people don't realize they see
their mirror image when they look into a sunset.*
The colours ran from orange to violet and then
to all sorts of greys.
I woke up realizing
I was supposed to say something
and could not.
Marian (the girl) looked like me
but with short blond hair.
She was most exuberant.

—ANNABELLE HÉBERT

MY BROTHER, BEAUTIFUL SHINAULT,
THAT GOAT

Me and my brother
always got burnt
in any kind of trade
like once I gave
Gilmer Hyatt half
a stamp collection
for two hamsters,
one fell out
of my pocket
on my way home,
the other one died
two days later,
but the worst was
Beautiful Shinault
getting that year-
old bicycle
off my brother
for a rusted-out
wagon and a goat
that was two-thirds
crazy, which one
day got loose
in the house
and busted up
a chair, five
dinner plates,
a window pane,
two canning jars,
and a screen door,

and after that
Mother said check
with her next
time we got to
feeling commercial-
minded.

—DAVID HUDDLE

MISS CREIGHTON

was, at the age of seventy, one
of the best single-handed farmers
we could think of. Alone, in
a long blue dress and high-top
shoes, she rode the mower hard
behind her two black horses,
raised her beef and cleared
her land of rocks.
                    "It does
good where I pick them up,"
she said, "and where I put
them down."
            And when,
one August day on top of her
hay wagon, she dropped
the fork and died, the horses
slowly turned and moved toward the barn.

—HENRY TAYLOR

HAY FOR THE HORSES

He had driven half the night
From far down San Joaquin
Through Mariposa, up the
Dangerous mountain roads,
And pulled in at eight a.m.
With his big truckload of hay
       behind the barn.
With winch and ropes and hooks
We stacked the bales up clean
To splintery redwood rafters
High in the dark, flecks of alfalfa
Whirling through shingle-cracks of light,
Itch of haydust in the
       sweaty shirt and shoes.
At lunchtime under Black oak
Out in the hot corral,
—The old mare nosing lunchpails,
Grasshoppers crackling in the weeds—
"I'm sixty-eight" he said,
"I first bucked hay when I was seventeen
I thought, that day I started,
I sure would hate to do this all my life
And dammit, that's just what
I've gone and done."

—GARY SNYDER

DOMESTIC QUARREL

The walls of the house are paper thin.
Lying awake in the pit of night
he hears his parents arguing,
and lights a candle stealthily.
The world's two halves are closing in
a sounding shell; the voices flicker,
knives that violate the night.
He lies imprisoned inside a whale,
his blind eyes trace its arching ribs.
The dark beats down.
Somewhere, offstage, ripples of distant thunder.
The window frames momentary bleached photographs,
cold as a moon landscape.
He blows the candle out and waits
for sleep or the consummation of rain
on the tin roof, the tides of drowning sound.

—SALLY MCINERNEY

POWWOW

(Tama Reservation, Iowa, 1949)

They all see the same movies.
  They shuffle on one leg,
    Scuffing the dust up,
  Shuffle on the other.
They are all the same:
  A Sioux dance to the spirits,
  A war dance by four Chippewa,
  A Dakota dance for rain.
    We wonder why we came.

Even tricked out in the various braveries—
  Black buffalo tassels, beadwork, or the brilliant
  Feathers at the head, at the buttocks—
Even in long braids and the gaudy face paints,
    They all dance with their eyes turned
  Inward, like a woman nursing
A sick child she already knows
  Will die. For the time, she nurses it
  All the same. The loudspeakers shriek;
    We leave our bleacher seats to wander
  Among the wickiups and lean-tos
In a search for hot dogs. The Indians
    Are already packing, have
  Resumed green dungarees and khaki,
  Castoff combat issues of World War II.
    (Only the Iroquois do not come here;
They work in structural steel; they have a contract
    Building the United Nations
  And Air Force installations for our future wars.)

These, though, have dismantled their hot-dog stand
            And have to drive all night
To jobs in truck stops and all-night filling stations.
            We ask directions and
        They scuttle away from us like moths.
            Past the trailers,
        Beyond us, one tepee is still shining
Over all the rest. Inside, circled by a ring
            Of children, in the glare
        Of one bare bulb, a shrunken fierce-eyed man
Squats at his drum, all bones and parchment,
            While his dry hands move
        On the drumhead, always drumming, always
Raising his toothless, drawn jaw to the light
        Like a young bird drinking, like a chained dog,
Howling his tribe's song for the restless young
            Who wander in and out.
            Words of such great age,
Not even he remembers what they mean.
            We tramp back to our car,
        Then nearly miss the highway, squinting
Through red and yellow splatterings on the windshield,
            The garish and beautiful remains
             Of grasshoppers and dragonflies
That go with us, that do not live again.

                      —W. D. SNODGRASS

KITCHEN DOOR BLUES

My old lady died
of a common cold.
She smoked cigars
and was ninety years old.

She was thin as paper
with the ribs of a kite
and she flew out the kitchen
door one night!

Now I'm no younger'n
the old lady was
when she lost gravitation
and I smoke cigars.

I look sort of peaked
and I feel kind of pore,
so for God's sake lock
that kitchen door!

—TENNESSEE WILLIAMS

THE FAT BOY'S DREAM

In a dream I open the door
And enter a room where ham grows on bone.
I pull back the chair and sit. Smoothing my napkin
In my lap, I look about and see I am alone.

I eat, my face close to the plate.
Bones, brains, liver, I devour the butcher's crime.
I drink from the fingerbowl, and no one looking,
I sharpen my knife on my fork as I dine.

Waking, I am huge, swollen, and floating far above.
My puffed cheeks are full, and painted red, like a clown's.
My parents enter the room, and shrieking, jump to tug at my foot,
But no one, no one, can ever bring me down.

—RICHARD MCCANN

TRAVELING
THROUGH THE DARK

STRANGE TREE

Away beyond the Jarboe house
    I saw a different kind of tree.
Its trunk was old and large and bent,
    And I could feel it look at me.

The road was going on and on
    Beyond, to reach some other place.
I saw a tree that looked at me,
    And yet it did not have a face.

It looked at me with all its limbs;
    It looked at me with all its bark.
The yellow wrinkles on its sides
    Were bent and dark.

And then I ran to get away,
    But when I stopped and turned to see,
The tree was bending to the side
    And leaning out to look at me.

—ELIZABETH MADOX ROBERTS

THE FISHER CAT

Wildness sleeps upon the mountain
And then it wakes in an animal
And in us, and in the sophistication of city streets
And in the danger of the indifferent murder,
We see the fisher cat on the limb of the tree,
Or is it a marten, or what is this slim, fierce beast
Caught in the flashlight's glare at night in Vermont,
Ready to leap at the baying dogs?

This enemy, this ancient foe, what is he?
The unexpected beast glares down from the high branch
Ready to pounce and fills man with fear,
Some nameless fear of millions of years ago in the forest,
Or the Rift valley in East Africa
When it was life or death in an instant.

The man has a gun, the instrument that has saved him,
Without which the drama of this intense moment
Might have ended in the death of man, and no poem;
He raised his piece like a violator of nature
And aiming at the jewelled caskets of the eyes
Brought the treasure trove of brain and sport.

The beast fell to the ground, unable to comment,
His beauty despoiled that took millions of years to grow.
The dogs thrashed around a while and quieted.
The New England hunter then with his matter of fact,
Taking for granted his situation mastery, put the
Mythic beast in the back of his four wheel drive vehicle.

It has taken the scientists of the university months
To decide what kind of an animal the creature was.
The centimeters of the back molars were counted,
Books were consulted, in the end it was decided,
Not by the scientist but by the poet, that a god
Had descended on man, and had to be killed.

Wildness sleeps upon the mountain
And when it wakes in us,
There is a perilous moment of stasis
When savagery meets equal savagery.
The long arm of man maintains intelligence
By death: his gun rang out instant doom.
The paws of the animal were very wide,
The claws of the beast were wide, long his thrashing tail.

—RICHARD EBERHART

THE TREES IN THE ROAD

The cliff gave way and the slope shifted ground,
The oaks rode upright and possessed the road
And what had been hanging changed its abode,
And to get beyond was to go around.

I wrought a path through the resettled wood,
Through boneset and rue and fever-cure bed,
Through self-heal and balm once over my head.
The conquering landslide was down for good.

The bloodroot bloomed early and broke the snow,
And I plucked the stems without climbing high,
And I dug the roots without mounting sky.
The wild from above was as wild below.

—JAMES STILL

MOSCHUS MOSCHIFERUS

A Song for St. Cecilia's Day

In the high jungle where Assam meets Tibet
The small Kastura, most archaic of deer,
Were driven in herds to cram the hunters' net
And slaughtered for the musk-pods which they bear;

But in those thickets of rhododendron and birch
The tiny creatures now grow hard to find.
Fewer and fewer survive each year. The search
Employs new means, more exquisite and refined:

The hunters now set out by two or three;
Each carries a bow and one a slender flute.
Deep in the forest the archers choose a tree
And climb; the piper squats against the root.

And there they wait until all trace of man
And rumour of his passage dies away.
They melt into the leaves and, while they scan
The glade below, their comrade starts to play.

Through those vast listening woods a tremulous skein
Of melody wavers, delicate and shrill:
Now dancing and now pensive, now a rain
Of pure, bright drops of sound and now the still,

Sad wailing of lament; from tune to tune
It winds and modulates without a pause;
The hunters hold their breath; the trance of noon
Grows tense; with its full power the music draws

A shadow from a juniper's darker shade;
Bright-eyed, with quivering muzzle and pricked ear,
The little musk-deer slips into the glade
Led by an ecstasy that conquers fear.

A wild enchantment lures him, step by step,
Into its net of crystalline sound, until
The leaves stir overhead, the bowstrings snap
And poisoned shafts bite sharp into the kill.

Then, as the victim shudders, leaps and falls,
The music soars to a delicious peak,
And on and on its silvery piping calls
Fresh spoil for the rewards the hunters seek.

But when the woods are emptied and the dusk
Draws in, the men climb down and count their prey,
Cut out the little glands that hold the musk
And leave the carcasses to rot away.

A hundred thousand or so are killed each year;
Cause and effect are very simply linked:
Rich scents demand the musk, and so the deer,
Its source, must soon, they say, become extinct.

Divine Cecilia, there is no more to say!
Of all who praised the power of music, few
Knew of these things. In honour of your day
Accept this song that I have made for you.

—A. D. HOPE

THE MURMURERS

They are formidable under any feather
and each name; of fly, of sharp sound, soft sound or flower:
oiseau-mouche, zum-zum, beija flor—these on the wing.
Their color? Science cries like a lover, of their light:
Heliomaster, Stellula, Chrysolampsis, Sapphira—sun
fire, star fire, torch fire, jewel fire in the air.

Honey, honey—what rapacity! All the air
vibrates with that passion. Ravage, ravage—wing
and beak and raging hunger plunge them, flower by flower,
along the raceme nodding balanced on the light;
the brief immortelle on its yellow great tree of sun,
hog-plum, ixora, wear like a nimbus their fire and feather.

At night, if they wish, they can die; but not quite. Feather-
light, lax, you may handle them, head limp, wing
elegantly shut. But dive up into blue air
at a moment. In 1653 Father Cobo taught the light
of the Resurrection to the Indians by that power. The sun
on their plumage might have served for the Trinity in flower,

requiring three in one—light, angle, eye, to flower
into their color; lacking one, they go colorless as air.
Interference is the cause of iridescence: feather-
shaft, barb and barbule—must have its sun
as seer; its color is structural, and light
knows this is not a pigment but a murmur of wing.

Water lovers, waterfall lovers, by wet wing
they go, pool shatterers, wet leaf drinkers, light-
ing on nothing; dew drainers, their drenched elected flower
magnetizes metal. Elliptical platelets, feather-
soft? goldsmith stuff inlaid with an eye to air?
Murmurers, feast, fight, flash in the Tobago sun!

Songless, belligerent, airy bone and feather,
seethes in their blood; the brilliant obedient air
frees them from patience, fear and commitment. Flower
or hawk they manoeuvre the murmurers: by wing, by wing
fight, feast, flash—as though the color's feather
on breast, racket tail, gorget, were an attribute of light.

Songless, belligerent, fierce fearless bone and feather,
the round sun like a fruit swells to draw your wing
and needle beak, and the whole island's flower is the sound of
    your light.

                                       —JOSEPHINE JACOBSEN

TRAVELING THROUGH THE DARK

Traveling through the dark I found a deer
dead on the edge of the Wilson River road.
It is usually best to roll them into the canyon:
that road is narrow; to swerve might make more dead.

By glow of the tail-light I stumbled back of the car
and stood by the heap, a doe, a recent killing;
she had stiffened already, almost cold.
I dragged her off; she was large in the belly.

My fingers touching her side brought me the reason—
her side was warm; her fawn lay there waiting,
alive, still, never to be born.
Beside that mountain road I hesitated.

The car aimed ahead its lowered parking lights;
under the hood purred the steady engine.
I stood in the glare of the warm exhaust turning red;
around our group I could hear the wilderness listen.

I thought hard for us all—my only swerving—,
then pushed her over the edge into the river.

—WILLIAM STAFFORD

THE FLOOD

It is good sometimes to grasp our helplessness.
We went one night to see them hold the levee.
The slope burned with torches; in light and dark
Men struggled, brown and white, with bags of sand,
Building the top, or below, where it seeped in a boil.

Fires hissed in the rain, a steady rain
Blown on gusts of wind from the raw west.
Waves lapped at the ridge, and as we looked
Reached higher and higher, land-enfolding arms.
In two days it broke and the home sirens screamed.

School was finished. Farmers poured to the town.
The protection levee was being closed. No one
Thought it could hold but the engineer, a man
Called Wright, who was always wrong; he had built
The city streets with ditches that bounced the cars—

His own device for drainage; in a flat land
They could never drain themselves. Widow Archer called
From her yard: "D'ye think he'll hold the water, Judge?"
"I doubt it," my father said. "He should," she cried,
"He's held it in our streets these twenty years."

Harder to keep it out than in; the river came,
Sat a while at the gates and then crept through.
Who could forget the longing of that night,
Or how, at the break of morning, down the street,
Those silver lanes of liquid ran like a dawn?

—CHARLES G. BELL

THE BLUE-HOLE

The swirl of water dominates the plain
Where water is exiled. They thought also
To straighten the river like a man-made thing.
When I first left on my grown wanderings,
They were cutting the necks across the oxbow bends.

I stand on a spur of the old levee now
Where it broke for the great flood. The river, wide
Before me, banked with swift willows, is curving
Again. The current down the straightening strikes
This shore, takes it visibly, slide by slide.

The double blue-hole that it broke and made,
Dug in the flat earth as a token well
Of waiting beneath all things, drawing the veil
Between the waters of the ground and sky,
Deep and filled with fish, tree-shadowed now,

Where the live river eats at the buckshot mud,
Attends that union—give it a year or more,
And the last bank will settle, the racing brown
Pour in the green depths, eager for those arms,
Homecoming always to the mother flood—

Not father of waters, deeper, deeper far:—
I was born of your dark dissolving, waited years
Firm-formed and clearing for the night's return,
The melting of all things, under cloud and rain,
And recessive evening drowned in the ocean of stars.

—CHARLES G. BELL

INDIAN CAMP

Smoke snakes
above each tepee.
The air is thick
heavy with dusk
and spirits.

All day it has rained.
Now the sky has come to earth
and the women
look at their hands
and their children
and their men walking through clouds.

The creek is close by.
Hurried and unheeded
it mumbles and mutters its name
lent of the Muskgoeans.

The old men
tell how the rocks
have souls.
They have seen the rain water
stand in the hollows
of their stone shoulders.

When the warriors die
they will be given
food and tools.
When these people are gone
they will have taken the land
with them.

—JANET REED MCFATTER

THE WIND HAS WINGS

Nunaptigne . . . In our land—*ahe, ahe, ee, ee, iee*—
The wind has wings, winter and summer.
It comes by night and it comes by day,
And children must fear it—*ahe, ahe, ee, ee, iee.*
In our land the nights are long,
And the spirits like to roam in the dark.
I've seen their faces, I've seen their eyes.
They are like ravens, hovering over the dead,
Their dark wings forming long shadows,
And children must fear them—*ahe, ahe, ee, ee, iee.*

—*Eskimo chant translated by*
  RAYMOND DE COCCOLA *and* PAUL KING

WITH HANDS LIKE LEAVES

The hounds sleep well. It is not they who stir the fox
And fret the owl; it is I, wandering on quiet feet.
It is I upon this high land sharpened by the moon.
I have gone softly, I have seen small eyes burn white
In thicket-dark, and I have heard sleep-twitters sound
Where the mulberry sheds its caterpillar fruit.

This is not a mountain I walk upon. It is a ridge
Of sleep or death, a slope hung on a night-jar's speech.
A child walks here with hands like leaves, with eyes
Like swifts that search the darkness in a perilous land.
He seeks a hill where living day shall stand.

—JAMES STILL

THE VERY
NEAREST ROOM:
Love Poems

ELYSIUM IS AS FAR AS TO

Elysium is as far as to
The very nearest Room
If in that Room a Friend await
Felicity or Doom—

What fortitude the Soul contains,
That it can so endure
The accent of a coming Foot—
The opening of a Door—

—EMILY DICKINSON

SONG FOR A COUNTRY WEDDING

For Deborah and Marc

We have come in the winter
To this warm country room,
The family and friends
Of the bride and the groom,
To bring them our blessing,
To share in their joy,
And to hope that years passing
The best measures employ
  To protect their small clearing,
  And their love be enduring.

May the hawk that flies over
These thick-wooded hills,
Where through tangled ground cover
With its cushion of quills
The plump porcupine ambles
And the deer come to browse
While through birches and brambles
Clear cold water flows,
  Protect their small clearing,
  And their love be enduring.

May the green leaves returning
To rock maples in spring
Catch fire, and, still burning,
Their flaming coat fling
On the lovers when sleeping
To contain the first chill
Of crisp autumn weather
With log-fires that will
  Protect their small clearing,
  And their love be enduring.

May the air that grows colder
Where the glacier has left
Its erratic boulder
Mountain water has cleft,
And the snow then descending
No less clear than their love
Be a white quilt depending
From sheer whiteness above
  To protect their small clearing,
  And their love be enduring.

   —WILLIAM JAY SMITH

AN IMMORALITY

Sing we for love and idleness,
Naught else is worth the having.

Though I have been in many a land,
There is naught else in living.

And I would rather have my sweet,
Though rose-leaves die of grieving,

Than do high deeds in Hungary
To pass all men's believing.

   —EZRA POUND

VALENTINE

Chipmunks jump, and
Greensnakes slither.
Rather burst than
Not be with her.

Bluebirds fight, but
Bears are stronger.
We've got fifty
Years or longer.

Hoptoads hop, but
Hogs are fatter.
Nothing else but
Us can matter.

—DONALD HALL

JUKE BOX LOVE SONG

I could take the Harlem night
And wrap around you,
Take the neon lights and make a crown,
Take the Lenox Avenue buses,
Taxis, subways,
And for your love song tone their rumble down.
Take Harlem's heartbeat,
Make a drumbeat,
Put it on a record, let it whirl,
And while we listen to it play,
Dance with you till day—
Dance with you, my sweet brown Harlem girl.

—LANGSTON HUGHES

THE SMALL

The small birds swirl around;
The high cicadas chirr;
A towhee pecks the ground;
I look at the first star:
My heart held to its joy,
This whole September day.

The moon goes to the full;
The moon goes slowly down;
The wood becomes a wall.
Far things draw closer in.
A wind moves through the grass,
Then all is as it was.

What rustles in the fern?
I feel my flesh divide.
Things lost in sleep return
As if out of my side,
On feet that make no sound
Over the sodden ground.

The small shapes drowse; I live
To woo the fearful small:
What moves in grass I love—
The dead will not lie still,
And things throw light on things,
And all the stones have wings.

—THEODORE ROETHKE

AS WELL AS THEY CAN

As well as it can, the hooked fish while it dies,
Gasping for life, threshing in terror and pain,
Its torn mouth parched, grit in its delicate eyes,
    Thinks of its pool again.

As well as he can, the poet, blind, betrayed
Distracted by the groaning mill, among
The jostle of slaves, the clatter, the lash of trade,
    Taps the pure source of song.

As well as I can, my heart in this bleak air,
The empty days, the waste nights since you went,
Recalls your warmth, your smile, the grace and stir
    That were its element.

          —A. D. HOPE

THE QUARREL

You sit behind your coffee.
I sit behind mine.
Our eyes are inside us.

Silence lies stale between us
on this morning whose heat is rent
by the singular shrill of a cicada.

And stale as a warped slice of bread is our quarrel,
and oppressive as this August morning is our love,
that mute as a moth with a torn wing,
lurches a path across the table.

          —KAREN SWENSON

SONNET: DOLCE STIL NOVO

(Esercitazione Letteraria)

That woman who to me seems most a woman
I do not compare to angels—or digress on schismatic Popes—
or exalt above the terrestrial or consider a madonna.
Nor do I search in others for her lineaments,
or wish for Death to free me from desire,
or consider Love an archer; or see her as a Daphne
fleeing the embraces of Apollo, transformed into a laurel.
I am not lost in the amorous wood of Virgil.

But although I do not rhyme or use the soft Italian,
my love is a strong love, and for a certain person.
Human beings are human: I can see a man might envy
her bath water as it envelops her completely.
That's what my love would like to do; and Petrarch
can take a running jump at himself—or (perhaps?) agree.

—GAVIN EWART

GIRAFFE AND TREE

Upon a dark ball spun in Time
 Stands a Giraffe beside a Tree:
Of what immortal stuff can that
 The fading picture be?

So, thought I, standing beside my love
 Whose hair, a small black flag,
Broke on the universal air
 With proud and lovely brag:

It waved among the silent hills,
 A wind of shining ebony
In Time's bright glass, where mirrored clear
 Stood the Giraffe beside a Tree.

—WALTER J. TURNER

POULTRY

"I thought you were a bird of paradise,
but you're just a silly goose."

G. B. SHAW

He set out snares,
his own heart as bait
for claws to tear,
his eager flesh in wait
for tropic air
of birds of paradise,
for proud arching neck,
for beaks, for hooded eyes.
What is this peck,
peck, peck?

—DIANA DER HOVANESSIAN

AT A SUMMER HOTEL

I am here with my beautiful bountiful downy womanful child,
to be soothed by the sea—not roused by these roses roving wild!
My girl is gold in the sun and bold in the dazzling water;
she drowses on the blond sand, and in the daisy fields my daughter
dreams. Uneasy in the drafty shade, I rock on the veranda,
reminded of Europa . . . Persephone . . . Miranda.

—ISABELLA GARDNER

PIAZZA DI SPAGNA,
EARLY MORNING

I can't forget
How she stood at the top of that long marble stair
Amazed, and then with a sleepy pirouette
Went dancing slowly down to the fountain-quieted square;

Nothing upon her face
But some impersonal loneliness, —not then a girl,
But as it were a reverie of the place,
A called-for falling glide and whirl;

As when a leaf, petal, or thin chip
Is drawn to the falls of a pool and, circling a moment above it,
Rides on over the lip—
Perfectly beautiful, perfectly ignorant of it.

—RICHARD WILBUR

THROUGH
A GREEN NIGHT:
Nature Poems

THE HERMIT WAKES TO BIRD SOUNDS

He startles awake. His eyes are full of white light.
In a minute the sun will ooze into the sky.
Meanwhile, all the machines of morning start up.

The typewriter bird is at it again.
Her style is full of endearing hesitations.
The words, when they come, do so in
the staccato rush of a deceitful loveletter.

The sewing machine bird returns to the doddering elm.
Like Penelope, she rips out yesterday's stitches
only to glide up and down, front and back
reentering the same needle holes.

The bird who presides at the wellhouse primes the pump.
Two gurgles, a pause, four squeaks of the handle
and time after time a promise of water
can be heard falling back in the pipe's throat.

Far off the logging birds saw into heartwood
with rusty blades, and the grouse cranks up
his eternally unstartable Model T
and the oilcan bird comes with his liquid pock pock

to attend to the flinty clanks of the disparate parts
and as the old bleached sun slips into position
slowly the teasing inept malfunctioning
one-of-a-kind machines fall silent.

—MAXINE KUMIN

CONSIDERING THE SNAIL

The snail pushes through a green
night, for the grass is heavy
with water and meets over
the bright path he makes, where rain
has darkened the earth's dark. He
moves in a wood of desire,

pale antlers barely stirring
as he hunts. I cannot tell
what power is at work, drenched there
with purpose, knowing nothing.
What is a snail's fury? All
I think is that if later

I parted the blades above
the tunnel and saw the thin
trail of broken white across
litter, I would never have
imagined the slow passion
to that deliberate progress.

—THOM GUNN

ON A SEA-GRAPE LEAF

*(Explorers in the West Indies
having no parchment, cut
messages on the leaves.)*

All I would say
Fills one leaf,
Love, grief,
Will to survive
The next turbulence,
Earth, waters,
Whirlwind, geysers,
Flame from the mountain
Ash along the shore.

To be alive
When the thin moon
Swings in sunset,
When trades rattle
Under palms.
To mount bony death
And scale the peak
Into dark
As the Southern Cross rises.

—KATHERINE GARRISON CHAPIN

THE SHEPHERD AND HIS FLOCK

The rays of the sun
are like a pair of scissors
cutting the blanket
of dawn from the sky.

The young shepherd
drives the master's sheep
from the paddock
into the veld.

His bare feet
kick the grass
and spill the dew
like diamonds
on a cutter's table.
A lamb strays away
enchanted by the marvels
of a summer morning;
the ram
rebukes the ewe,
"Woman! Woman!
Watch over the child!"

The sun wings up
on flaming petals
of a sunflower.

He perches on an antheap
to play the reed flute,
and to salute
the farmer's children
going to school,
and dreamily asks,
"O! Wise Sun above,
will you ever guide
me into school?"

—OSWALD MBUYISENI MTSHALI

BOUQUET IN DOG TIME

A bit of yarrow and then of rue
steeplebush and black-eyed susan
one fringed orchis, ragged and wry
some meadowsweet, the vetch that's blue
to make a comeliness for you
with dogbane, daisies, bouncing bet
the clover red, the clover white
walking the field before the night
lazy under a lavender sky
(crazy and spent in the race with fear)
for one of every kind that's here
sundew, burnet, thimbleberry
all so simple, all so true
like a bit of yarrow and of rue.

—HAYDEN CARRUTH

SIX HAIKU

For Graham V. Phillips Who First Said the First One

1.
"The cat spreads herself
across my bed, like pea
-nut butter on bread."

2.
Tow-head dandelions,
gray heads by end of August.
So soon we vanish!

3.
That silver balloon,
the moon, drifts free of Him
whose breath gave it shape.

4.
That early riser,
the sun, stands on a footstool
to observe the day.

5.
Pluck a daisy here—
elsewhere in the universe
a great star trembles.

6.
To write too many
haiku is to be nibbled
to death by small fish.

—ROBERT PHILLIPS

DUTCH APRIL

Tulips charge the grazing dikes, and I walk
In wood along canals, the water
Creeping from street to street where old men talk
Herring days. The breath of every flower
Hangs a scent on the air like laundry,
Each color boxed with its pedigree
Nailed against the wind. These colors recur
Like familiar faces on wine evenings.

A tulip Sunday: dresses are wings
Beating beyond my reach. In the sweet wake
The fish women swoon in their reverse make-
Up, hawking sardines fresh from the North Sea.

A lighter, poled from still water, springs
Its load of ripe Edam upon the quay.

—DANIEL HALPERN

RIVER

The river moans.
The river sings.

Listen to the Fox, the Menominee,
The Susquehanna, Colorado, Platte,
The Ottawa, Snake, Bear,
And the Delaware.

Listen to the river.
The river moans.
The river sings.

The river is always going home.

—LAWRENCE LOCKE

THE ROUND

Skunk cabbage, bloodroot,
ginseng, spring beauty,
Dutchman's-breeches,
rue, and betony;

bluets, columbine,
cowslip and bittercress,
heartleaf, anemone,
lupin, arbutus;

bunchberry, merrybells,
Jack-in-the-pulpit,
hepatica, vetch,
and dogtooth violet;

pussy-willow, starwort,
wet-dog trillium,
alumroot, lady's-slipper,
Solomon's-plume;

milkweed, fireweed,
loosestrife and dogbane,
sunbright, buttercup,
thistle, and pipevine;

paintbrush, bunchlily,
chicory, candy-root,
spatterdock, sundew,
touch-me-not;

goldenrod, aster,
burdock and coral-
root, gentian, ragweed,
jumpseed, and sorrel;

upland yellow-eye
and Joe-pye-weed,
bittersweet, sumac,
snow, and frozen seed.

—PHILIP BOOTH

SPRING

Not all of us were warm, not all of us.
We are winter-lean, our faces are sharp with cold
And there is a smell of wood smoke in our clothes;
Not all of us were warm, though we hugged the fire
Through the long chilled nights.

　　　　　　We have come out
Into the sun again, we have untied our knot
Of flesh: We are no thinner than a hound or mare,
Or an unleaved poplar. We have come through
To the grass, to the cows calving in the lot.

—JAMES STILL

SUNFLOWER

Sunflower, of flowers
the most lonely,
yardstick of hours,
long-term stander
in empty spaces,
shunner of bowers,
indolent bender
seldom, in only
the sharpest of showers:
tell us, why
is it your face is
a snarl of jet swirls
and gold arrows, a burning
old lion face high
in a cornflower sky,
yet by turning
your head, we find
you wear a girl's
bonnet behind?

—JOHN UPDIKE

RAIN ON THE CUMBERLANDS

Through the stricken air, through the buttonwood balls
Suspended on twig-strings, the rain fog circles and swallows,
Climbs the shallow plates of bark, the grooved trunks,
And wind-pellets go hurrying through the leaves.
Down, down the rain; down in plunging streaks
Of watered grey.

Rain on the beachwood trees. Rain upon the wanderer
Whose breath lies cold upon the mountainside,
Caught up with broken horns within the nettled grass,
With hoofs relinquished on the breathing stones
Eaten with rain-strokes.

Rain has buried her seed and her dead.
They spring together in this fertile air
Loud with thunder.

—JAMES STILL

TAMARACK

The tamarack tree is the saddest tree of all;
it is the first tree to invade the swamp,
and when it makes the soil dry enough,
the other trees come and kill it.
It is very much abused.
It cannot grow in shade,
is put upon by parasite growths:
witches' broom and the dwarf mistletoe.

—EUGENE MCCARTHY

TRENCH

Reptiles move like Navajo beadwork
Across the sand suggesting water maybe,
The sun glinting off rippling snakes
Or twisting lizards leaving shallow stream beds
Empty like a punch line through the sage.
Mule tongues hang fat and dripping
Beneath fired eyes as though stretched
And licking the moisture from the air thinned
And drying. Their faces are like wagon planks
With knots for eyes. There is no spine
To the horizon, the land is dead with white hands
Pointing nowhere like cactus. And water shows
Its smooth forehead time upon time only to burrow
Quickly creasing the sand. They dig with blistered fingers
Oozing into the dunes to sink into sleep into a cool
Pothole the size of a wagon wheel in shade almost.

—STEPHEN PETT

AMONG THE FINGER LAKES

These great brown hills move in herds, humped like bison,
before the travelling eye. Massive above the farms, they file
and hulk daylong across every distance; and bending come
as the sun sinks (orange and small) beyond their heavy shoulders,
shaggy at evening, to drink among the shadowy lakes.

—ROBERT WALLACE

SINKHOLES

If they made any noise in forming,
I can't remember.
But I like to think the ground opened
silently, like a fist.

Often the holes came at night.
In the morning, the ground dropped away,
roots dangled into a toothless mouth.
I thought then no place secure,

as I peered into trapped water
where my face looked back, eyeless,
a small death's head designed like mine.

Now, as then, in rear view mirrors, windows
I have seen my face, with misgiving,
reflected back.

And at night, before sleep,
I remember how the ground gave way,
and my throat becomes a dark tunnel,
air sinks into the caves of my hips,
the hollows of my shoulders, and I know
that at my going
the earth will silently open,
silently close.

—JANET REED MCFATTER

THE OPEN SEA

We say the sea is lonely; better say
Ourselves are lonesome creatures whom the sea
Gives neither yes nor no for company.

Oh, there are people, all right, settled in the sea;
It is as populous as Maine today,
But no one who will give you the time of day.

A man who asks there of his family
Or a friend or teacher gets a cold reply
Or finds him dead against that vast majority.

Nor does it signify that people who stay
Very long, bereaved or not, at the edge of the sea
Hear the drowned folk call: that is mere fancy,

They are speechless. And the famous noise of sea
Which a poet has beautifully told us in our day
Is hardly a sound to speak comfort to the lonely.

Although not yet a man given to prayer, I pray
For each creature lost since the start at sea,
And give thanks it was not I, nor yet one close to me.

—WILLIAM MEREDITH

REMEMBERING

AEGEAN

Where only flowers fret
And some small passionate
Bird sings, the trumpets sounded yesterday.
The famous ships are gone,
Troy fades, and the face that shone—
Fair Helen, in her tower—could not stay.

Where are the temples set
Their gods would not forget,
The trophies, and the altars? Echo, say.
There's no one anymore
But Echo on the shore,
And Echo only laughs and runs away.

Though still the olive glows
Like silver, and the rose
Is glittering and fresh, as in their day,
No witnesses remain
Of battles on the plain
And the bright oar and the oar spray.

—LOUIS SIMPSON

GRANDMOTHER, ROCKING

Last night I dreamed of an old lover,
I had not seen him in forty years.
When I awoke,
I saw him on the street:
his hair was white
his back stooped.
How could I say hello?
He would have been puzzled all day
about who the young girl was
who smiled at him.
So I let him go on his way.

—EVE MERRIAM

THE DEPOT

(Midwest, 19th century)

The rails pause barely to tie the horizons
where the wheatfields curve into day and night.
A wooden cart, long-handled and iron-wheeled,
stands in shadow under the baggage sign.
Dust settles in the road on the other side.

The great hand hides the small
on the face of the town hall tower.
Behind the ticket-window grill
there is small disagreement:
the railroad's time depends and seldom falters.

A valise lies on the green bench
upon the platform:
the planks show their weathers.
A locust buzzes in a cindered elm.
The door blisters and stands ajar.

A hawk whose shadow crosses the tracks
can see the pigeon's lighter gray
against the slate, the iron flue.
The dirt track follows the rails,
then turns north among the fields.

Houses diminish; now and then
a silo pierces the yellows and rusts.
There may be a thunderhead
somewhere at the edge of things.
There may be smoke and a thin sound.

—LEWIS TURCO

PIANO

Softly, in the dusk, a woman is singing to me;
Taking me back down the vista of years, till I see
A child sitting under the piano, in the boom of the tingling
  strings
And pressing the small, poised feet of a mother who smiles as she
  sings.

In spite of myself, the insidious mastery of song
Betrays me back, till the heart of me weeps to belong
To the old Sunday evenings at home, with winter outside
And hymns in the cozy parlor, the tinkling piano our guide.

So now it is vain for the singer to burst into clamor
With the great black piano appassionato. The glamour
Of childish days is upon me, my manhood is cast
Down in the flood of remembrance, I weep like a child for the
  past.

—D. H. LAWRENCE

SONG FROM A COUNTRY FAIR

When tunes jigged nimbler than the blood
And quick and high the bows would prance
And every fiddle string would burst
To catch what's lost beyond the string,
While half afraid their children stood,
I saw the old come out to dance.
The heart is not so light at first,
But heavy like a bough in spring.

—LÉONIE ADAMS

MEMOIRS OF A SPINACH–PICKER

They called the place Lookout Farm.
                              Back then, the sun
Didn't go down in such a hurry. How it
Lit things, that lamp of the Possible!
                              Wet yet
Lay over the leaves like a clear cellophane,
A pane of dragonfly wing, when they left me
With a hundred bushel baskets on the edge
Of the spinach patch.
                    Bunch after bunch of green
Upstanding spinach-tips wedged in a circle—
Layer on layer, and you had a basket
Irreproachable as any lettuce head,
Pure leafage. A hundred baskets by day's end.

Sun and sky mirrored the green of the spinach.
In the tin pail shaded by yellow paper
Well-water kept cool at the start of the rows.
The water had an iron taste, and the air,
Even, a tang of metal.
                    Day in, day out,
I bent over the plants in my leather-kneed
Dungarees, proud as a lady in a sea
Of prize roses, culling the fullest florets;
My world pyramided with laden baskets.

I'd only to set one foot in wilderness—
A whole sea of spinach-heads leaned to my hand.

—SYLVIA PLATH

MY GRANDADDY MOSTLY WITH HIS KNIFE

Balanced a row of peas on it
all the way up to his mouth;
poured coffee cup to saucer
and back until it got cool;
sat back smoking and told us
how at mealtime Uncle Dave
and his daddy had had terrible
arguments about that war
the one had fought in
and the other hadn't,
how Uncle Bill threw a cat
in a crock of liver pudding dough,
how he'd fired a train
back and forth between Roanoke
and Charlestown, West Virginia;
had a pocket watch he'd check
every time he heard a whistle;
drank pretty heavy of an evening
and promised to take me with him
to Bristol and buy me a gold
cornet but never got around to it;
sat after dark in the study,
Grandmama behind him listening
to Lowell Thomas with her eyes
shut and nodding her head;
wrote stuff on the backs
of old envelopes: chemical formulae,
algebra problems, names of hotels;
said he was just trying
to remember what he'd forgotten;

told me to go practice my music;
tried to whistle for me
even though he was tone deaf
the only tune he ever much liked:
There'll Be A Hot Time
In The Old Town
Tonight.

—DAVID HUDDLE

FIRST SNOW

The old black dog comes in one evening
with the first few snowflakes on his back
and falls asleep, throwing his bad leg out
at our excitement. This is the night
when one of us gets to say, as if it were news,
that no two snowflakes are ever alike;
the night when each of us remembers something
snowier. The kitchen is a kindergarten
steamy with stories. The dog gets stiffly up
and limps away, seeking a quiet spot
at the heart of the house. Outside,
in silence, with diamonds in his fur,
the winter night curls round the legs of the trees,
sleepily blinking snowflakes from his lashes.

—TED KOOSER

REFLECTION: AFTER VISITING OLD FRIENDS

To touch all points in the past
is to stretch your life like a skin
to the breaking. In Tuscaloosa
with friends the old stories are replayed
like traffic or stock car races:
crash and terminal circling.
We sit on the sofa like spectators.
On the freeways, headlines are being made.

In scrub pine, purple martins give way
to April; the slow migration completed.
Mosquito larvae in a near pond wiggle
to the surface for air, for wing.
The wind a sure carburetion.
Inside we breathe through our skins.

—JOHN ALLISON

BATTLE WON IS LOST

They said, "You are no longer a lad."
      I nodded.
They said, "Enter the council lodge."
      I sat.
They said, "Our lands are at stake."
      I scowled.
They said, "We are at war."
      I hated.
They said, "Prepare red war symbols."
      I painted.
They said, "Count coups."
      I scalped.
They said, "You'll see friends die."
      I cringed.
They said, "Desperate warriors fight best."
      I charged.
They said, "Some will be wounded."
      I bled.
They said, "To die is glorious."
      They lied.

—PHIL GEORGE

RETURN OF THE PRODIGAL SON (conclusion)

Elephant of Moissel, hear my pious prayer.
Give me the fervent science of Timbuktu's great doctors.
Give me the will of Soni Ali, son of the Lion's foam, a tidal
    wave to conquer a continent.

Breathe on me the wisdom of the Keitas.
Give me the Guelwar's courage and gird my lions with a Tyédo's
    strength.
Let me die for the cause of my people, in the stink of gun and
    cannon if need be.
May the love of this people stay fast and take root in my liberated
    heart.
Make me your Master of Language; no, make me his ambassador.

Blessed be my fathers, who bless the Prodigal!
I want to see the women's house again, I played there with the
    doves and my brothers, the sons of the Lion.
Ah! To sleep once again in my childhood's cool bed,
Tucked in once again by the black hands so dear,
And once more the white smile of my mother.

Tomorrow I set out again for Europe, on the diplomatic path,
Homesick for the Black Land.

—LÉOPOLD SÉDAR SENGHOR

(translated from the French by Ellen Conroy Kennedy)

THOSE WINTER SUNDAYS

Sundays too my father got up early
and put his clothes on in the blueblack cold,
then with cracked hands that ached
from labor in the weekday weather made
banked fires blaze. No one ever thanked him.

I'd wake and hear the cold splintering, breaking.
When the rooms were warm, he'd call,
and slowly I would rise and dress,
fearing the chronic angers of that house,

Speaking indifferently to him,
who had driven out the cold
and polished my good shoes as well.
What did I know, what did I know
of love's austere and lonely offices?

—ROBERT HAYDEN

RAIN

How mobile is the bed on these
nights of gesticulating trees
    when the rain clatters fast,
the tin-toy rain with dapper hoof
trotting upon an endless roof,
    travelling into the past.

Upon old roads the steeds of rain
slip and slow down and speed again
    through many a tangled year,
but they can never reach the last
dip at the bottom of the past,
    because the sun is there.

—VLADIMIR NABOKOV

PACKET OF LETTERS

In the shut drawer, even now, they rave and grieve—
To be approached at times with the frightened tear;
Their cold to be drawn away from, as one, at nightfall,
Draws the cloak closer against the cold of the marsh.

There, there, the thugs of the heart did murder.
There, still in murderers' guise, two stand embraced, embalmed.

—LOUISE BOGAN

WORLD WINTER

WORLD WINTER

Sun
proud Bessemer   peltwarmer beauty
these winters yoke us   We scan sky for you
The dun droppings blue   we drown in snow
Is this tarnished chimneyplug   in a tenantless room
this sucked wafer   white simpleton
you?

Not
chiefly the months   mould you heartcharmer
to scant hammerdent   on hardiron sky
not alone latitude   to lodgers on this
your slantwhirling lackey   lifecrusted satellite
this your one wrynecked   woedealing
world

—EARLE BIRNEY

NOTHING GOLD CAN STAY

Nature's first green is gold,
Her hardest hue to hold.
Her early leaf's a flower;
But only so an hour.
Then leaf subsides to leaf.
So Eden sank to grief,
So dawn goes down to day.
Nothing gold can stay.

—ROBERT FROST

COME WITH ME INTO WINTER'S
DISHEVELED GRASS

Come with me into winter's disheveled grass.
Bittersweet beads against the unhinged and barren apple tree.
Inside its gored trunk a last wad of snow lingers.

I give you a burr spined like a sea urchin.
You give me the split womb of the milkweed.

Together we will gather the hunter's cartridges
strewn across the frozen earth.
Red for you.
Green for me.
How the cylinders glow their hollows in the sun
now that death is gone.

—KAREN SWENSON

WINTER

I am entrenched
Against the snow,
Visor lowered
To blunt its blow

I am where I go

—SAMUEL MENASHE

STOPPING BY WOODS ON A SNOWY EVENING

Whose woods these are I think I know.
His house is in the village, though;
He will not see me stopping here
To watch his woods fill up with snow.

My little horse must think it queer
To stop without a farmhouse near
Between the woods and frozen lake
The darkest evening of the year.

He gives his harness bells a shake
To ask if there is some mistake.
The only other sound's the sweep
Of easy wind and downy flake.

The woods are lovely, dark, and deep,
But I have promises to keep,
And miles to go before I sleep,
And miles to go before I sleep.

—ROBERT FROST

READING IN FALL RAIN

The fields are black once more.
The old restlessness is going.
I reach out with open arms
to pull in the black fields.

All morning rain has fallen
steadily on the roof.
I feel like a butterfly
joyful in its powerful cocoon.

*

I break off reading:
one of my bodies is gone!
It's outdoors, walking
swiftly away in the rain!

I get up and look out.
Sure enough, I see
the rooster lifting his legs
high in the wet grass.

—ROBERT BLY

LYNX

His fur resembles waves
of leaves, under which a wind

is heaving. White
and dry, his lighter hair

seems nearer winter,
scattered across his coat

like frosted straw. Beneath
his mouth, like ice beneath

a crevice, lies
his beard. It is as cold

as the white rings around
his eyes, which now begin

to close, as might
the rings of frost around

a stem: the mouth
of winter.

—BEN HOWARD

THE SNOWFISH

As oceans are to porpoises
The snowdrift to the snowfish is.
The snowfish swims down with the snow
And tunnels in the drifts below.

Some creatures move in air or mud,
Moles in earth and worms in wood,
Owls in hollow trunks of trees:
Many the shapes of nature's fancies.

His various fishy cousins swim
In water for a medium.
These he resembles more or less
In iridescent nakedness.

Little about him can be taught
By scientific schools of thought.
He does not seem to fit the rules
That work for those who swim in schools.

And though great numbers of him fall
The snowfish won't conform at all.
The photograph you try to take
Will melt him quicker than a snowflake.

You cannot catch him with a line:
When thickets of snow are coming down
You know the snowfish is around
By the knocking on your windowblind,

But that's the only sound he makes—
Music makes him dance a bit;
Most of all he loves good wit,
But he's never taken any bait.

All we can say of him is this:
He must be accepted as he is;
You must allow him to exist:
He might be something you have missed.

To each a season when he sleeps;
To each a weather when he goes.
Today's the day when wise men see
The snowfish frisking in the snow.

—EDWARD FIELD

COMPOSITION IN BLACK AND WHITE

All day long they have sat here
black monosyllables, crows on a bare tree
while the hills slowed under snow,
becoming the fields, and the fields,
their sodden stubble of wheat
blanked over, leaned toward earth.

My heart rejoices as it can
and finds haphazard grace
in any mobile thing: I praise
these heavy fields, but more
the abrupt rising of crows
who flew up with a cry, their brilliant blacks
astonishing the air
as they scattered
leaving each branch sprung
taut, alive like wires.

—KATHA POLLITT

WEEDS

Nothing so startles us as tumbleweeds in December
Rising like ghosts before us in the headlamps
The big round weeds blowing into fences
Into guard rails and wheels, wedged into corners
Drifting in ranks over roads in a gusty order
Round in the orbits of winter, dropping the invisible seed,
Blown green and purple-leaved into springtime, soft with water,
Filled to harsh circles in the thirsty summer
Dried brown and jagged, ready for December
When the silver globes, magnificent in procession
Slow and solemn-paced in the ritual of ending
Dry, dead, in the dim-most part of the year
Spread the great round promises of green morning.

—ANN STANFORD

QUESTIONING FACES

The winter owl banked just in time to pass
And save herself from breaking window glass.
And her wings straining suddenly aspread
Caught color from the last of evening red
In a display of underdown and quill
To glassed-in children at the window sill.

—ROBERT FROST

MORNING PRAYER

Now another day is breaking,
Sleep was sweet and so is waking.
Dear Lord, I promised you last night
Never again to sulk or fight.
Such vows are easier to keep
When a child is sound asleep.
Today, O Lord, for your dear sake,
I'll try to keep them when awake.

—OGDEN NASH

POET'S WISH

When I have been dead for several years
And cabs in the fog still collide
As they do today (things not having changed)
May I be a cool hand upon some forehead!
On the forehead of someone humming in a carriage
Along Brompton Road, Marylebone or Holborn,
Who, thinking of literature,
Looks out through the yellow fog at the great black monuments.
Yes, may I be the dark, gentle thought
One bears secretly in the noise of cities,
A moment's repose in the wind that drives us on,
Lost children in this vanity fair;
And may my humble beginning in eternity be honored
On All Saint's Day with a simple ornament, a little moss.

—VALERY LARBAUD

(translated from the French by William Jay Smith)

AUTHOR INDEX

TRANSLATOR INDEX

TITLE INDEX

WILLIAM JAY SMITH

poet, critic, and translator, is the author of *The Traveler's Tree: New and Selected Poems* and *Army Brat: A Memoir*, which tells about his growing up as the son of an enlisted man in the Regular Army. Mr. Smith has written a number of books of poetry for children, including the popular *Laughing Time*. He compiled, with the late Louise Bogan, the celebrated anthology *The Golden Journey*. His poems have appeared in anthologies throughout the English-speaking world.

JACQUES HNIZDOVSKY

is a well-known painter and printmaker. He is an acknowledged master of the woodcut and has illustrated the poetry of Keats, Coleridge, and Thomas Hardy. His work hangs in the Boston Museum of Fine Arts, the Philadelphia Museum of Art, and The White House. Born in the Ukraine, he now lives in New York with his wife and daughter.